托福写

TOEFL writing
vocabulary by subject

场景词汇

新航道托福研发中心 / 编著

LIFESTYLE EMPLOYMENT Work and Success
Personal Character SO Education and Study
the Media Ac ce and Technol
Entertainmer CANDIDATE PROMOTI
LOYALTY Domestic Temperament Indiffere
Invent Herbiv forestation

精准释义

覆盖**8大常考场景**
精选**900个主题词条**

搭配**场景例句**

同根+同义+反义，扩大词汇量
巩固练习，即学即用

世界知识出版社

图书在版编目（CIP）数据

托福写作场景词汇 / 新航道托福研发中心编著 . — 北京：
世界知识出版社，2018.8
ISBN 978-7-5012-5828-4

Ⅰ . ①托… Ⅱ . ①新… Ⅲ . ① TOEFL － 写作 － 自学参考
资料 Ⅳ . ① H315
中国版本图书馆 CIP 数据核字（2018）第 187593 号

策划编辑	马凤祥　付玉燕
责任编辑	龚玲琳
文字编辑	蔡楚娇
责任出版	王勇刚
责任校对	马莉娜
书　　名	托福写作场景词汇 Tuofu Xiezuo Changjing Cihui
编　　著	新航道托福研发中心
出版发行	世界知识出版社
地址邮编	北京市东城区干面胡同 51 号（100010）
网　　址	www.ishizhi.cn
电　　话	010-65265923（发行）　010-85119023（邮购）
经　　销	新华书店
印　　刷	三河市富华印刷包装有限公司
开本印张	880×1230 毫米　1/32　10 印张
字　　数	278 千字
版次印次	2018 年 8 月第 1 版　2018 年 8 月第 1 次印刷
标准书号	ISBN 978-7-5012-5828-4
定　　价	32.00 元

新航道图书编委会

主　　任　胡　敏

委　　员　（按姓氏笔画为序）

马凤祥　　冉　维

李传伟　　陈　红

陈采霞　　杨　宏

胡　敏　　顾　强

蔡　政　　[美]彭铁城

本册编著　徐天祥

前言

　　编者在教学过程中发现，很多考生在准备托福写作时经常会遇到两个令人头疼的问题：一是想好了思路，可是不知道用什么单词准确、形象地表达出来；二是写出来的词太过简单或单调，更像是大白话而不是写作语言。这两个问题，在独立写作部分暴露得尤为明显。

　　其实，这些问题都是词汇输入量不够造成的。写作考查的是考生的输出技能，但输出的前提是大量的输入。可是输入什么呢？托福写作考试对于词汇的要求并不是很高，在清楚地表达出自己观点的基础上，词汇使用丰富、符合用语习惯即可。但是这项要求对于中国考生来说并非易事，因为国内的英语考试系统对于写作的要求很低，与托福考试要求的水平有明显的差距，这就导致考生写托福作文时词汇匮乏、短语枯竭、中式英语频现。要知道，我们的托福作文是要拿给美国考官评分的，如果作文词汇水平都不符合考试要求，又如何打动甚至让他们看懂呢？于是，出于周围越来越多的考生对写作，尤其是独立写作的词汇资料的迫切需求，这本专门为托福写作打造的场景词汇书便应运而生了。

　　为了使本书真正做到与时俱进，更好地服务于托福考生，编者对常考的独立写作场景进行了分类，具体归纳为教育与学习、工作与成功、生活方式等八大类。此外，为了满足不同考生的需求，编者还特别总结归纳出写作高频替换词和高分短语。其中写作高频替换词可以帮助考生解决因重复使用某些词汇而无法展示出词汇丰富性的问题；高分短语则为大家补充地道的、有一定文采的语料，为考生的作文增光添彩。最后，为了巩固单词的记忆，每个章节后面都有相关的练习板块，即学即练，加深印象。具体来说，本书在编排上具有以下几大特色：

1. 覆盖八大常考场景，精选 900 个核心词条

本书涉及的独立写作场景有八大类，涵盖了目前考试的所有场景，收录核心词条 900 个，包括词性的变体衍生词、短语搭配和固定用法等，让考生学完一个单词，不仅马上就会用，而且还能举一反三，掌握与该词词源相同的衍生词。

2. 精准释义搭配场景例句

书中收录的词条释义，在具体场景中尽量体现此场景下的常考词性、常考意义，其中每一词条的第一义项皆配有权威英文词典中的例句，且例句难度适中，不仅展示了该词条的具体使用，还包含了一些实用短语，甚至有的例句可以直接用在独立写作中。鉴于我们写作时通常先在头脑中想到对应的中文表达，然后再把它翻译成英文，所以，本书把这样的思维过程在编著的时候体现了出来。也就是说，读者先会看到中文例句、词组，然后看到对应的英文例句、搭配。

3. 巩固练习，即学即用

本书每个章节都设置了课后练习板块，包括词汇背诵检查和句子理解练习。其中很多句子都选自独立写作常用的句型，搭配本章节的核心词条，二者相互补充，使考生学完单词会写句子，写完句子记住单词。

4. 附赠地道美音 MP3 下载

我们为本书配备了标准的美音 MP3 音频文件，包含所收词条以及例句。读者可以到新航道图书官方手机 APP 嗨书免费下载。

希望本书能够帮助考生在写作考试中做到准确、地道和丰富的表达，正所谓"下笔如有神，篇篇出高分"。祝愿每一位拿到此书的读者都有一个美好的、享受的阅读体验。

编者
2018 年 8 月

目录

第一章

教育与学习

相 关 词 汇

curiosity [ˌkjʊriˈɑːsəti]

释义· *n.* 好奇心；奇物；珍品

例句· 实地考察旅行可以激起学生们的好奇心。

The field trips can kindle the curiosity of the students.

同根· curious *adj.* 好奇的

搭配· 激起好奇心 kindle curiosity

appeal [əˈpiːl]

释义· *v.* 有吸引力；上诉 *n.* 吸引力；呼吁；上诉

例句· 这本书的内容很有趣，吸引了很多学生购买。

The content of the book is very interesting and appeals to many students to buy.

派生· appealing *adj.* 有吸引力的

搭配· 请求；要求 appeal for

呼吁某人做某事 appeal to sb. to do sth.

assignment [ə'saɪnmənt]

释义· *n.* 作业；分配；任务

例句· 现在学生们每天都要做很多作业。

Now the students do a lot of school assignments every day.

搭配· 一项特殊的任务 a special assignment

parenting ['perəntɪŋ]

释义· *n.* (U)（父母对子女的）养育

例句· 良好的教养对孩子的未来大有裨益。

A sound parenting is a great benefit to the future of children.

搭配· 教养有方 / 无方 good/poor parenting

moral ['mɔːrəl]

释义· *adj.* 道德的；品行端正的 *n.* 道德；寓意

例句· 他们深入询问了她一些有关伦理学和逻辑学的问题。

They asked her some searching questions on moral philosophy and logic.

派生· morality *n.* 道德

prime [praɪm]

释义· *adj.* 首要的；主要的；最好的 *n.* (*sing.*) 全盛时期 *v.* 做准备

例句· 增加对教育的投资是现阶段的首要问题。

To increase the investment in education is the prime issue at the present stage.

同义· primary *adj.* 主要的；初级的；基本的

搭配· 黄金时间 prime time

最佳品质 prime quality

首相；总理 prime minister

使某人做好准备做某事 prime sb. to do sth.

一个典型的例子　a prime example

tuition [tu'ɪʃn]

释义· *n.* (U) 学费；讲课

例句· 大多数家庭负担不起日益增长的高昂学费。

Most families can't afford growingly expensive tuition.

peer [pɪr]

释义· *n.* 同龄人；贵族 *v.* 盯着看；凝视

例句· 他出色的表达能力使他在同龄人中出类拔萃。

His excellent presentation skill made him outstanding in peers.

搭配· 对等的　peer to peer

凝视　peer at

elite [eɪ'liːt]

释义· *n.* 精英；上层人士

例句· 许多大学生想成为精英，但他们当中只有极少数人愿意付出比别人更多的努力。

Many university students want to be elite, but very few of them would pay more effort than others.

搭配· 名校；精英学校　elite school

deviate ['diːvieɪt]

释义· *v.* 偏离；背离

例句· 考试作弊的人偏离了一项重要的社会价值观念：诚信。

People who cheat in the exam deviate from a significant social value: honesty.

搭配· 从……偏离　deviate from

rear [rɪr]

释义· v. 培养 n. 后面；屁股 adj. 后面的

例句· 他的母亲将他培养成了一个正直的人。

His mother reared him as an honest man.

humanities [hjuːˈmænətiz]

释义· n. (pl.) 人文学科

例句· 人文学科和社会科学是大学课程中最重要的两门学科。

The humanities and the social sciences are the two most important subjects in the university curriculum.

diploma [dɪˈploʊmə]

释义· n. 毕业证书

例句· 他提早完成学业，成功地拿到了毕业证书。

He finished his study in advance and got his diploma successfully.

scholarship [ˈskɑːlərʃɪp]

释义· n. 奖学金；学问

例句· 高额奖学金对学生们来说是一份不小的诱惑。

A high scholarship is an allure to the students.

adolescent [ˌædəˈlesnt]

释义· n. 青少年 adj. 青春期的

例句· 在许多国家，酒吧禁止青少年进入。

In many countries, the adolescent is banned from entering bars.

同义· teenager/juvenile/youths n. 青少年

同根· adolescence n. 青春期

feedback ['fiːdbæk]

释义· *n.* (U) 反馈；成果；回复

例句· 测试结果对学生们的学习效果有很好的反馈。

Test result gives students good feedback on the outcome of their study.

teamwork ['tiːmwɜːrk]

释义· *n.* 团队合作

例句· 分小组做实验或者研究项目可以培养学生们的团队合作意识。

Doing experiments or research projects in small groups can cultivate the teamwork of the students.

搭配· 团队精神　teamwork spirit

ignore [ɪgˈnɔːr]

释义· *vt.* 忽视；不予理睬

例句· 现在许多学校都忽视了学生的道德教育。

Now many schools have ignored the moral education of the students.

派生· ignorance *n.* 无知；愚昧

搭配· 忽视……的事实　ignore the fact that

mimic ['mɪmɪk]

释义· *vt.* 模仿 *n.* 模仿者

例句· 小孩子善于模仿但无法明辨是非。

The children are good at mimicking but cannot distinguish between right and wrong.

同义· imitate *vt.* 模仿

扩展· mimicked (过去式) mimicked (过去分词)

pedagogical [ˌpedəˈgɑːdʒɪkl]

释义· *adj.* 教学法的

例句· 如今，教师们的教学方法日益地个性化。

Nowadays, teachers' pedagogical methods are becoming more and more individualized.

同根· pedagogy *n.* 教育学；教学法

搭配· 教学方法 pedagogical method

adversity [ədˈvɜːrsəti]

释义· *n.* 逆境

例句· 青少年只有在逆境中成长，才能在遇到困难时无所畏惧。

Only when teenagers grow in adversity can they be fearless in the face of difficulties.

mental [ˈmentl]

释义· *adj.* 精神的；智力的

例句· 约翰的目标是考上哈佛大学，这给他造成了很大的心理压力。

John's target is to be admitted to Harvard University, which caused heavy mental pressure on him.

同义· psychological *adj.* 精神上的；心理的

派生· mentality *n.* 心态；思想状况

搭配· 心理健康 mental health

铭记 make a mental note

attend [əˈtend]

释义· *v.* 出席；参加；照顾

例句· 几乎没有人来上这位教授的公开课。

Few people attend this professor's open class.

派生· attendance *n.* 出席；参加

搭配· 上课 attend a course

照料某人 / 某物 attend to sb./sth.

outline ['aʊtlaɪn]

释义· *n.* 大纲；轮廓 *vt.* 概述；显示……的轮廓

例句· 我花了一个月的时间完成了我的论文大纲。

It took me a month to finish the outline for my paper.

搭配· 概括地；扼要地 in outline

generalist ['dʒenrəlɪst]

释义· *n.* 全才；多面手

例句· 现在的教育注重培养全才。

The present education pays attention to cultivate of generalists.

specialist ['speʃəlɪst]

释义· *n.* 专家 *adj.* 专业的；专家的

例句· 专家在哪个领域都受欢迎，尤其是在高尖端科技领域。

Specialists are popular in all domains, especially in the field of high cutting-edge technology.

同根· specialize *v.* 专门从事

discipline ['dɪsəplɪn]

释义· *n.* 学科；纪律；训练 *v.* 训练；惩戒

例句· 社会学是一门相对较新的学科。

Sociology is a relatively new discipline.

搭配· 某人严格要求自己做某事 discipline oneself to do sth.

校纪 school discipline

curriculum [kəˈrɪkjələm]

释义· *n.* （学校等的）全部课程

例句· 总课程的设置一般都是全国统一的。

In general, the curriculum is unified throughout the country.

同义· course *n.* （一门）课程

扩展· curricula/curriculums (*pl.*)

vocational [voʊˈkeɪʃənl]

释义· *adj.* 职业的

例句· 这门课程旨在提供工程方面的职业培训。

This course is designed to provide vocational training in engineering.

搭配· 职业学校 vocational school

职业教育 vocational education

dull [dʌl]

释义· *adj.* 无趣的；迟钝的 *vt.* 使迟钝；使阴暗

例句· 教授们常常会试着讲些生动有趣的例子，好让课堂内容显得不那么无趣。

Professors often try to make some interesting examples, so that the content of the lecture is not so dull.

depend [dɪˈpend]

释义· *v.* 依靠；取决于

例句· 如果你想获得一个好成绩，仅仅依靠老师上课教授的内容是很难的。

If you want to get a good grade, it is difficult to depend on the teacher's content solely.

派生· dependent *adj.* 依赖的

dependency *n.* 依赖；附属国

搭配· 取决于；依赖　depend on

obedience [əˈbiːdiəns]

释义· *n.* (U) 服从

例句· 通过这次测试，学生们学会了真正的服从和尊重。

Via this test, students have learnt true obedience and deference.

搭配· 绝对 / 无条件服从　complete/unquestioning obedience

pride [praɪd]

释义· *n.* (U) 骄傲；自豪；自尊心 *v.* 自豪

例句· 骄兵必败。

Pride goes before a fall.

搭配· 以……为傲　pride in

qualified [ˈkwɑːlɪfaɪd]

释义· *adj.* 合格的；有资格的

例句· 经过讨论，大多数人认为他有资格加入这所学校，成为一名合格的英语口语教师。

After discussion, most people think he is qualified to join the school and become a qualified Oral English teacher.

反义· unqualified *adj.* 不合格的；不胜任的

搭配· 有担任……的资格　be qualified for sth.

rewarding [rɪˈwɔːrdɪŋ]

释义· *adj.* 值得做的；有益的；报酬高的

例句· 她的小说构思精妙、情节复杂，值得一读。

Her novels are so intricate and exquisite that they are rewarding to read.

schooling [ˈskuːlɪŋ]

释义· *n.* (U) 学校教育

例句· 从这个大学生的行为举止上人们可以看出他受过良好的教育。

It can be seen from the behavior of the college student that he has received good schooling.

syllabus [ˈsɪləbəs]

释义· *n.* 教学大纲

例句· 当看到这份大纲上再次写满了要读的书时，他突然意识到自己已经三个月没有休息了。

When seeing the syllabus filled with books again, he suddenly realized that he had no rest for three months.

vigor [ˈvɪgər]

释义· *n.* (U) 活力；精力

例句· 互联网的出现给教育和金融业带来了新的活力，但是与此同时也衍生出了各种各样的问题。

The emergence of the Internet has brought new vigor to the education and the financial industry, but at the same time, a variety of problems have been derived.

派生· vigorous *adj.* 精力充沛的

unify [ˈjuːnɪfaɪ]

释义· *v.* 统一；使成一体

例句· 不同的省份有着不同的教科书和评分标准，有人认为这有失公平，应该尽快统一。

Different provinces have different textbooks and grading standards. Some people think it is unfair and should be unified as soon as possible.

派生· unification *n.* 合一；联合；统一

proficient [prəˈfɪʃnt]

释义· *adj.* 精通的；熟练的

例句· 这位教授精通英语和模型涂装。

The professor is proficient in English and model painting.

派生· proficiency *n.* 精通；熟练

搭配· 精通于…… be proficient in/at

master [ˈmæstər]

释义· *v.* 精通；控制 *adj.* 最重要的；熟练的 *n.* 主人

例句· 这位博学多才的教授打小就精通多种语言。

The versatile professor can master a variety of languages since childhood.

搭配· 擅长（某物）be a past master (at sth.)

精通……的能手 be a master of

硕士学位 master's degree

mature [məˈtʃʊr]

释义· *adj.* 成熟的；成年的 *v.* 成熟

例句· 虽然他已经是成年人了，但他的独立思考能力还不够成熟。

Although he is already an adult, his ability of independent thinking is not mature enough.

搭配· 经过深思熟虑 on mature reflection/consideration

critical [ˈkrɪtɪkl]

释义· *adj.* 批判性的；极重要的；危险的

例句· 学校应该注重从小就培养学生的批判性思维。

School should emphasize the cultivation of student's critical thinking from an early stage.

搭配· 批判性思维 critical thinking

（尤指针对具体事由）批评某人 / 某事 be critical of sb./sth.

open-minded [ˌoʊpən ˈmaɪndɪd]

释义· *adj.* 思想开放的；虚心的

例句· 组内的良性竞争可以加强孩子们的团队合作精神、沟通能力，并使他们的思想更加开阔。

Benign competition within the group can promote children's teamwork spirit, communication skills, and make them open-minded.

反义· narrow-minded *adj.* 狭隘的；心胸狭窄的

credit [ˈkredɪt]

释义· *n.* 学分；信用；贷款 *vt.* 相信；把……归于

例句· 修不够足够的学分学生就无法毕业。

Without enough credits, students cannot graduate.

搭配· 赊账 on credit

把……归功于某人 / 某物 be credited to sb./sth.

信用卡 credit card

lecture [ˈlektʃər]

释义· *n.* 讲座；演讲；教训 *v.* 讲课；指责

例句· 综合写作通常要求你先阅读一篇学术文章，然后听一篇相关内容的课堂讲义。

Integrated writing often requires you to read a passage about an academic topic and listen to a lecture about the same topic.

派生· lecturer *n.* 讲师；演讲者

搭配· 有关……的演讲 lecture on

acquaint [əˈkweɪnt]

释义· v. 使熟悉，使了解

例句· 大一新生应该熟知校园的地图，否则会经常找不到上课的教室。

First-year students should be acquainted with the maps of the campus, or they often fail to find the classroom.

派生· acquaintance n. 熟人

搭配· 把某事告知某人　acquaint sb. with sth.

熟悉……　be acquainted with

indulge [ɪnˈdʌldʒ]

释义· v. 沉溺；满足；放纵

例句· 他沉溺于这道难题无法自拔，已经三天没有睡觉了。

He indulged in this conundrum so that he hadn't slept for three days.

派生· indulgence n. 嗜好；纵容

搭配· 沉溺于某事　indulge in sth.

bully [ˈbʊli]

释义· v. 欺负；霸凌；威吓 n. 仗势欺人者

例句· 高年级学生欺负低年级学生的现象在校园里很普遍。

It is very common in the campus that senior students bully junior students.

扩展· bullied（过去式）bullied（过去分词）

enlighten [ɪnˈlaɪtn]

释义· v. 启发；开导

例句· 他不仅解放了这个地区的农民，还开化、教育、帮助了他们。

Not only did he emancipate the farmers in the region, but also helped, enlightened and educated them.

派生· enlightened *adj.* 开明的

enlightening *adj.* 有启发作用的；启发人的

搭配· 就某事启发某人 enlighten sb. as to/on/about sth.

astray [əˈstreɪ]

释义· *adv.* 误入歧途地

例句· 年少时他曾误入歧途，上了大学后，他意识到了学习的重要性。

He had gone astray when young, and after going to college, he was aware of the importance of learning.

搭配· 误入歧途；偏离正轨 go astray

alienated [ˈeɪliəneɪtɪd]

释义· *adj.* 疏远的

例句· 在又一次的争吵之后，他觉得自己和父母的关系越发地疏远了。

After another quarrel, he felt more and more alienated from his parents.

seminar [ˈsemɪnɑːr]

释义· *n.* 研讨会；研讨课

例句· 学校要求学生在每周二的研讨会上提交一份上周的学习报告。

The school requires students to submit last week's work report at the seminar on every Tuesday.

stomach [ˈstʌmək]

释义· *v.* 忍受

例句· 成为一名运动员的道路是漫长而艰辛的，他们往往需要忍受高强度的训练和极大的心理压力。

The path to an athlete is long and hard, and they often have to stomach high strength training and heavy psychological pressure.

同义· tolerate/abide v. 忍受

cultivate [ˈkʌltɪveɪt]

释义· vt. 培养；陶冶；耕作

例句· 很多人都不知道，其实政府已经拨出了人均三万元的大学生教育补贴来培养人才。

In fact, the government has subsidized 30,000 yuan per capita to cultivate college talents.

派生· cultivated *adj.* 有教养的

搭配· 培养人才 cultivate talents

instill [ɪnˈstɪl]

释义· vt. 灌输

例句· 教师不仅要向学生灌输知识，还要教他们待人处事的方法。

Teachers are asked not only to instill knowledge into students but also to teach them how to treat people.

搭配· 向某人灌输某物 instill sth. in/into sb.

impart [ɪmˈpɑːrt]

释义· v. 传授；通知；给予（特指抽象事物）

例句· 他教给了这个孩子一个更简单的解题方法。

He imparts the child a more straightforward method to solve the problem.

搭配· 传授；将……给予 impart to

mold [moʊld]

释义· vt. 塑造

例句· 一个好的老师应帮助孩子形成自己的性格。

A good teacher helps mold a child's character.

mentor ['mentɔːr]

释义· *n.* 导师；顾问

例句· 直到 1915 年他去世为止，他一直是她的良师益友。

He was her friend and mentor until his death in 1915.

同义· tutor *n.* 导师；家庭教师 *v.* 辅导

counselor ['kaʊnsələr]

释义· *n.* 顾问；辅导老师

例句· 我们的顾问是一位善于书法的长者。

Our counselor is an elder who is good at calligraphy.

guardian ['gɑːrdiən]

释义· *n.* 监护人；保护者

例句· 一般来说，未成年人的监护人是他们的父母。

In general, parents are the guardians of juveniles.

academic [ˌækə'demɪk]

释义· *adj.* 学业的；学术的

例句· 他优异的学习成绩对他申请硕士学位起到了关键性作用。

His excellent academic record played a vital role in the application of the master degree.

搭配· 学业表现 / 学习成绩 academic performance/record

comprehensive [ˌkɑːmprɪ'hensɪv]

释义· *adj.* 综合的；广泛的；有理解力的

例句· 九年义务教育的目的之一是提高孩子们的综合素质。

One of the purposes of the nine-year compulsory education is to improve the comprehensive quality of the children.

同根· comprehensible *adj.* 可理解的

搭配· 综合素质 comprehensive quality

enrich [ɪnˈrɪtʃ]

释义· *vt.* 使丰富；使富足

例句· 高科技的迅速发展丰富了我们的学习方式。

The rapid development of high-technology has enriched our learning method.

派生· enrichment *n.* 丰富

搭配· 丰富生活 enrich life

provoke [prəˈvoʊk]

释义· *v.* 激起；驱使；激怒；煽动

例句· 这道复杂的数学题在教师们中引起了激烈的争论。

This complex mathematical problem has provoked fierce debate among teachers.

合成· thought-provoking *adj.* 引人深思的

搭配· 引起某人做某事 provoke sb. to do sth.

激怒某人（做）某事 provoke sb. into (doing) sth.

docile [ˈdɑːsl]

释义· *adj.* 容易教的；温顺的

例句· 这孩子很好管，老师们都很喜欢她。

This child is very docile, and teachers like her very much.

派生· docility *n.* 温顺

perplex [pərˈpleks]

释义· *vt.* 使困惑；使复杂

例句· 这门复杂的计算机科学课程让这个班所有学生都感到难以应付。

This complicated computer science course perplexed every student in this class.

派生· perplexing *adj.* 令人费解的

perplexed *adj.* 困惑的；迷惑不解的

overwhelm [ˌoʊvərˈwelm]

释义· *v.* 压倒；淹没；覆盖

例句· 我的弟弟被他的英语老师布置的大量作业压得喘不过气来。

My little brother was overwhelmed by tons of homework assigned by his English teacher.

派生· overwhelming *adj.* 势不可挡的；压倒性的

搭配· 被……压垮 be overwhelmed by

nerd [nɜːrd]

释义· *n.* 书呆子

例句· 在每个对书呆子绘声绘色的定义中，你都能找到怪咖的影子。

For every great definition of nerd, you can find the same definition of geek.

diversity [daɪˈvɜːrsəti]

释义· *n.* 多样性；差异

例句· 一个文明的国家往往能接受并融合不同文化的多样性。

A civilized country is often capable of accepting and mixing the diversity of different cultures.

同根· diverse *adj.* 不同的，变化多的

diversify *vt.* 使多样化

搭配· 文化多样性 cultural diversity

insightful [ˈɪnsaɪtfʊl]

释义· *adj.* 富有洞察力的；有深刻见解的

例句· 这位富有洞察力的教授很快就从一些小细节中发现了父母对孩子的体罚。

This insightful professor quickly found the parents' physical punishment of the child from some small details.

undertake [ˌʌndər'teɪk]

释义· vt. 保证；承担；从事；同意

例句· 我不能保证完成这本书，但我会尽力而为。
I can't undertake to finish this book, but I will do my best.

搭配· 承诺做某事；答应做某事 undertake to do sth.

扩展· undertook（过去式）undertaken（过去分词）

obligation [ˌɑːblɪ'geɪʃn]

释义· n. 义务；职责

例句· 老师布置作业时，学生通常认为完成作业是一种义务。
When teachers assign homework, students usually feel an obligation to do it.

同根· obliged adj. 感谢；感激

compulsory [kəm'pʌlsəri]

释义· adj. 义务的；必须的

例句· 九年义务教育是国家予以保障的教育事业。
The nine-year compulsory education is an educational cause guaranteed by the state.

搭配· 义务教育 compulsory education
必修课 compulsory course

adaptive [ə'dæptɪv]

释义· adj. 适应的；有适应能力的

例句· 为了更好地适应社会，很多高中生开始在暑假打工或做兼职。
To be better adaptive to the society, many high school students begin to work in the summer vacation or do part-

time jobs.

同根· adaptation *n.* 适应；改编

horizon [həˈraɪzn]

释义· *n.* 眼界；范围；地平线

例句· 随着眼界的不断开阔，这些新观念会为生活赋予全新的意义。

As your horizons expand, these new ideas can give a whole new meaning to life.

派生· horizontal *adj.* 水平的

搭配· 开阔某人的眼界 broaden/widen one's horizons

realize [ˈriːəlaɪz]

释义· *vt.* 实现；意识到

例句· 我们努力帮助所有的学生充分发挥他们的潜力。

We try to help all students realize their full potential.

搭配· 开始意识到 come to realize

authority [əˈθɔːrəti]

释义· *n.* 权威；权力；当局

例句· 他不惧权威，写下了这篇揭露当局黑暗面的批判性文章。

He can defy the authority and writes down this critical article to reveal the dark side.

派生· authoritative *adj.* 权威式的；命令式的；当局的

搭配· 在某人的许可下 under the authority of sb.

有关……的权威；……的专家 be an authority on

discriminate [dɪˈskrɪmɪneɪt]

释义· *v.* 歧视；辨别

例句· 一位教育工作者不应该因为学生有身体上的缺陷而歧视他。

An educator should not discriminate against any student

because of the physical defects.

派生· discrimination *n.* 歧视；区别；辨别

搭配· 歧视 discriminate against

versatile ['vɜ:rsətl]

释义· *adj.* 多才多艺的；多功能的；多面手的

例句· 这位多才多艺的老师在台上高歌了一曲，惊艳四座。

This versatile teacher sang a song loudly, astonishing the audience.

派生· versatility *n.* 多功能性；用途广泛；多才多艺

搭配· 通才 a versatile person

integration [ˌɪntɪ'greɪʃn]

释义· *n.* 结合；融合

例句· 教育是知识、技能和道德培养的结合。

Education is the integration of knowledge, skills and morality training.

同根· integrated *adj.* 综合的；完整的

sense [sens]

释义· *n.* 感觉；理智；意义 *v.* 感觉到

例句· 养宠物可以培养孩子强烈的责任感。

Raising a pet can cultivate a strong sense of responsibility for a child.

搭配· 有意义；讲得通 make sense

在某种意义上 in a sense

强烈的……感 a strong sense of

competence ['kɑ:mpɪtəns]

释义· *n.* 能力

例句· 大学教育可以提高年轻人的能力。

University education can enhance the competence of young adults.

acute [ə'kju:t]

释义· *adj.* 严重的；敏锐的；强烈的

例句· 明明面临这么严重的问题，他却想要当作什么都没发生过一样。

Faced with such an acute problem, he wanted to pretend nothing happened.

派生· acuteness *n.* 剧烈；敏锐

搭配· 剧痛 acute pain

一个严重的问题 an acute problem

diligent ['dɪlɪdʒənt]

释义· *adj.* 勤奋的；用功的

例句· 这位勤奋的教授经常利用课余时间阅读英文书籍，最近正准备写书了。

This diligent professor often used spare time to read English books, and was about to write books recently.

派生· diligence *n.* 勤奋

搭配· 勤勉于…… be diligent in

contribution [ˌkɑːntrɪ'bjuːʃn]

释义· *n.* 贡献；捐献；稿件

例句· 网络的发展对远程教育做出了巨大的贡献。

The development of the network has made a significant contribution to the distance education.

搭配· 做贡献 make a contribution

rote [rəʊt]

释义· *n.* (U) 生搬硬套；死记硬背

例句· 这篇生搬硬套的作文经常被他拿出来当作反例。

He usually takes this rote essay as a bad example.

搭配· 死记硬背 rote learning

bias ['baɪəs]

释义· *n.* 偏见 *vt.* 使有偏见

例句· 她曾经认为他所教授的解题思路烦琐而难懂，后来实践起来才发现这只是她的偏见。

She used to think that the idea he taught was tedious and difficult to understand, and after practice, she realized that it was only her bias.

派生· biased *adj.* 有偏见的

搭配· 偏斜地，倾斜地 on the bias

gap [gæp]

释义· *n.* 差距；间隙；缺口；分歧

例句· 汤姆通过努力逐渐缩小了与他最好朋友在学习成绩上的差距。

Through great effort, Tom bridged the gap of the academic results with his best friend.

搭配· 缩小差距 bridge the gap

时间差 time gap

性别差异 gender gap

endeavor [ɪn'devər]

释义· *n.* 努力 *v.* 努力；尽力

例句· 人们将成功归功于他的外表，而忽视他的努力。

People attribute success to his appearance but ignore his

endeavor.

distract [dɪ'strækt]

释义· *vt.* 分心；转移

例句· 智能手机上的游戏经常会使孩子们在做作业时分心。

Games on the smartphone often distract children from homework.

派生· distracted *adj.* 思想不集中的；心烦意乱的

distracting *adj.* 令人分心的

搭配· 转移；使从……分心　distract from

practice ['præktɪs]

释义· *n.* 实践；练习；惯例 *v.* 练习

例句· 实践出真知。

Genuine knowledge comes from practice.

派生· practical *adj.* 实际的；实用性的

搭配· 在实践中；实际上　in practice

实施；实行　into practice

intelligence [ɪn'telɪdʒəns]

释义· *n.* (U) 智力；情报

例句· 他认为标准化教育对那些智力水平低于或超出平均水平的儿童没有好处。

He feels the standardized education does not benefit those children who are either below or above average intelligence.

同根· intelligent *adj.* 智能的；聪明的

internship ['ɪntɜːrnʃɪp]

释义· *n.* 实习期

例句· 实习期结束后，他顺利留任。

After the internship, he retained successfully.

figure ['fɪgjər]

释义· *v.* 认为；计算 *n.* 数字；人物；图形

例句· 她觉得自己和内德都从这一经历中学到了很多东西。

She figured that both she and Ned had learned a lot from the experience.

搭配· 想出；计算出 figure out

谋取；企图获得 figure for

社会名人；公众人物 a public figure

interaction [ˌɪntərˈækʃn]

释义· *n.* 互动；相互作用

例句· 现在的教师更关注课堂上与学生的互动，而不是一个人从头讲到尾。

Now teachers focus on the interaction with students in their class rather than the monologue from beginning to end.

同根· interactive *adj.* 交互式的；相互影响的

搭配· 与……相互作用 interaction with

capable ['keɪpəbl]

释义· *adj.* 有能力的；能干的；有才能的

例句· 他讲座的内容太过高深，不是专业人士的话会感到难以理解。

The content of his lecture is so profound that non-professionals are not capable of comprehending.

反义· incapable *adj.* 没能力的

搭配· 有能力做某事 be capable of doing sth.

verbal ['vɜːrbl]

释义· *adj.* 口头的；言语的；文字的

例句· 他以出色的写作和口头表达能力在比赛中名列前茅。

He came top in the match for his excellent writing and verbal skills.

派生· verbalize *v.* 用言语表达

搭配· 语言能力 verbal skills

context ['kɑːntekst]

释义· *n.* 上下文；环境

例句· 通读上下文有助于更好地理解这句话的涵义。

Reading context helps to understand the meaning of this sentence better.

搭配· 在……的背景下 in the context of

脱离背景地复述某事 take/quote sth. out of context

core [kɔːr]

释义· *n.* 核心；要点

例句· 她具有能够深入问题本质的能力，总能从根源上发现问题。

She can analyze the core of matters, always finding problems from the root.

搭配· 内核 inner core

在……的中心 at the core of

hypothesis [haɪˈpɑːθəsɪs]

释义· *n.* 假设

例句· 他提出的假设都被一一推翻了。

His hypotheses are retorted one by one.

派生· hypothesize *v.* 假设；假定

扩展· hypotheses (*pl.*)

obscure [əb'skjʊr]

释义· *adj.* 晦涩的；难懂的；无名的 *vt.* 使模糊；使费解

例句· 这本晦涩难懂的书已在图书馆的角落里尘封多年了。

This obscure book has been sealed in the corner of the library for many years.

派生· obscureness *n.* 难解；模糊

interest ['ɪntrəst]

释义· *n.* 爱好；兴趣；利息 *vt.* 使感兴趣

例句· 他在米尔菲尔德私立学校上学的时候培养了广泛的运动爱好。

He developed a wide range of sporting interests as a pupil at Millfield.

搭配· 对某人有吸引力 be of interest to sb.

利率 interest rate

vivid ['vɪvɪd]

释义· *adj.* 生动的；鲜明的

例句· 他用生动诙谐的语言描述了自己儿时的趣事，调节了课堂气氛。

He described his interesting stories in childhood with humorous and vivid language, regulating the atmosphere of the class.

派生· vividness *n.* 生动；活泼

搭配· 一幅栩栩如生的画面 a vivid picture

accessibility [əkˌsesə'bɪləti]

释义· *n.* 易得到的；易使用的；易到达的

例句· 研讨会内容的选择是以普通听众容易理解为依据的。

Seminar topics are chosen for their accessibility to a general audience.

同根· accessible *adj.* 可接近的；容易理解的；可进入的

expertise [ˌekspɜːrˈtiːz]

释义· *n.* 专长；专门知识

例句· 他特别擅长数学，经常问老师们一些难题。

He has expertise in math, often asking some difficult questions to his teachers.

acquisitive [əˈkwɪzətɪv]

释义· *adj.* 渴望得到的；迫切求取的；贪婪的

例句· 他的求知欲是如此强烈，这里几乎没有一本书是他没有看过的。

His thirst for knowledge is so acquisitive that there is almost no book he has never seen.

派生· acquisition *n.* 获得；收购

term [tɜːrm]

释义· *n.* 学期；术语；期限；条款

例句· 许多学生抗议是因为这个学期学校提高了学费。

Many students protested because in this term the school raised the tuition.

搭配· 就……而言 in terms of

在……方面 in...terms

rigorous [ˈrɪgərəs]

释义· *adj.* 严格的；严厉的

例句· 他的成功归功于老师严格的要求。

He owes his success to his teacher's rigorous standards.

implication [ˌɪmplɪˈkeɪʃn]

释义· *n.* 暗示；含意；影响

例句· 从学生的暗示中老师了解到，他来自一个单亲家庭。

Teachers realized from this student's implication that he came from a single-parent family.

abandon [ə'bændən]

释义· vt. 放弃；遗弃 n. (U) 放任

例句· 因为家里没钱，他放弃了上大学的念头。

He abandoned the idea of going to college because of poverty.

派生· abandoned adj. 被抛弃的；放纵的

搭配· 沉溺于 abandon oneself to

不考虑后果；轻率 with gay abandon

behave [bɪ'heɪv]

释义· v. 表现；守规矩；举止得体；运转

例句· 今天汤姆的儿子在课上表现很好，老师当着全班同学的面表扬了他。

Today Tom's son behaved well in class, and teachers praised him in front of his classmates.

合成· well-behaved adj. 彬彬有礼的

搭配· 表现得体；有礼貌 behave oneself

optimist ['ɑːptɪmɪst]

释义· n. 乐观主义者

例句· 乐观者会在不幸中看到机遇，而悲观者则在机遇中看到不幸。

An optimist sees an opportunity in every calamity; a pessimist sees a disaster in every opportunity.

linguistic [lɪŋ'gwɪstɪk]

释义· adj. 语言的；语言学的

例句· 语言的发展对于我们研究人类起源是不可或缺的。

Linguistic development is indispensable to study the origin of human beings.

派生· linguistics *n.* 语言学

搭配· 语言能力 linguistic ability

gifted ['gɪftɪd]

释义· *adj.* 有天赋的；有天才的

例句· 这名老师天生具备幽默感，所以学生们都很喜欢他。

This teacher is gifted with humor, so he is popular among students.

搭配· 具有…… be gifted with

一名资优生 a gifted student

deliberate [dɪ'lɪbərət]

释义· *adj.* 深思熟虑的；故意的

例句· 为了避免犯错，她做每一个决定都是深思熟虑的。

To avoid error, she made each decision in deliberate.

派生· deliberately *adv.* 不慌不忙地；小心翼翼地

characteristic [ˌkærəktə'rɪstɪk]

释义· *n.* 特征；特色 *adj.* 典型的；特有的

例句· 成功者的一个重要特征就是要有良好的沟通能力。

One of the important characteristics of winners is to have good communication skills.

同根· characterize *vt.* 描述……的特性；具有……的特征

internal [ɪn'tɜːrnl]

释义· *adj.* 内部的；里面的

例句· 学习的内在动力是为了得到更好的未来。

The internal motivation for learning is to have a better future.

反义· external *adj.* 外在的

搭配· 内力 internal force

persistence [pər'sɪstəns]

释义· *n.* 坚持不懈；持续存在；毅力

例句· 学习的过程是枯燥无味的，所以必须坚持不懈。

The process of learning is uninteresting; therefore, you need persistence.

同根· persistent *adj.* 执著的；不屈不挠的

stifle ['staɪfl]

释义· *v.* 扼杀；窒息；压制

例句· 应试教育会扼杀孩子们的想象力。

Exam-oriented education will stifle the imagination of children.

派生· stifling *adj.* 令人窒息的；沉闷的

creativity [ˌkriːeɪ'tɪvəti]

释义· *n.* 创造力

例句· 教师们如何才能改进教学以激发创造性呢？

How can the faculty improve their teaching to encourage creativity?

同根· creative *adj.* 创造性的

theoretical [ˌθiːə'retɪkl]

释义· *adj.* 理论的；理论上的

例句· 埃米发现理论和笔头作业对她来说十分容易。

Amy discovered that the theoretical and written work came easily to her.

派生· theoretically *adv.* 理论上

psychological [ˌsaɪkə'lɑːdʒɪkl]

释义· *adj.* 心理的；心理学的

例句· 上一场比赛的胜利使他们比对手有心理优势。

Victory in the last game gave them a psychological advantage over their opponents.

同根· psychologist *n.* 心理学家

thesis ['θiːsɪs]

释义· *n.* 论文；论点

例句· 这学期末的时间太紧了，我都不确定能不能按时提交我的毕业论文。

It's too tight at the end of the semester. I'm not sure I can submit my graduation thesis on time.

搭配· 论文写作 thesis writing

学期论文 term thesis

bibliography [ˌbɪbli'ɑːgrəfi]

释义· *n.* 参考书目；文献目录

例句· 我刚刚用 Kindle 把教授参考书目里要求看的书都下载下来了。

I've just downloaded all the books in Kindle that the professor asked in the bibliographies.

patriotism ['peɪtriətɪzəm]

释义· *n.* (U) 爱国主义

例句· 每个国家都重视对学生进行爱国主义教育。

Every country attaches great importance to the education of patriotism for students.

同根· patriotic *adj.* 爱国的

foster ['fɔːstər]

释义· *adj.* 寄养的；代养的 *v.* 培养；代养

例句· 这个孩子来自寄养家庭，因为他的父母从小就抛弃了他。

The child came from a foster family because his parents had abandoned him since childhood.

搭配· 代养母 / 父 a foster mother/father

代养的家庭 / 寄养家庭 a foster family/home

寄养照管 foster care

motivation [ˌmoʊtɪ'veɪʃn]

释义· *n.* 动力；诱因

例句· 现在很多大学生缺乏进行科学研究的动力。

Now many university students lack the motivation to do scientific research.

派生· motivational *adj.* 动机的；动力的

literacy ['lɪtərəsi]

释义· *n.* (U) 读写能力

例句· 有声读物不仅能给他们带来娱乐，还能提高他们的读写能力。

Audio books will not only offer them entertainment, but also improve their literacy.

反义· illiteracy *n.* 文盲

搭配· 识字率 literacy rate

controversial [ˌkɑːntrə'vɜːrʃl]

释义· *adj.* 有争议的；有争论的

例句· 这两个人针对这个充满争议的答案讨论了半天。

The two men discussed this controversial answer for half a day.

反义· non-controversial/uncontroversial *adj.* 无争议的

revise [rɪ'vaɪz]

释义· *v.* 修改；修订；复习

例句· 我们需要修改课本中有关语言学部分的内容。

We need to revise the content of our textbook about the linguistics part.

派生· revised *adj.* 经过修订的

revision *n.* 修改；复习

搭配· （考前）复习……功课 revise for

scope [skoʊp]

释义· *n.* 范围；机会 *vt.* 仔细看

例句· 这些问题不属于本文论述范围。

These issues were outside the scope of the article.

搭配· 知识面 scope of knowledge

在……范围内 within the scope of

超出……范围 beyond the scope of

supervise ['suːpərvaɪz]

释义· *v.* 监督；指导

例句· 老师们密切监督着考场上学生们的一举一动。

Teachers are supervising each movement of students in the examination room.

派生· supervisor *n.* 监督人

supervision *n.* 管理；监督

常 用 短 语

释义	短语
小学	primary/elementary school
中学	secondary school
高中	high school
社区工作	community work
选修课	optional course
必修课	required course
基础科学	basic science
人文科学；文科	liberal arts
人文与科学的结合	marriage of humanities and sciences
课外活动	extra-curricular activities
给……机会	open the door to
学士学位	bachelor's degree
博士学位	Ph.D. (Doctor of Philosophy)
研究生	graduate student/postgraduate
就业技能	employable/marketable skills
中国高考	China's National College Entrance Examination
逻辑思维	logical thinking

明辨是非	differentiate virtue from evil
出国学习；留学	study overseas
挖掘某人的潜能	tap one's potential
旷课	drop/cut a class
缩小；限制	narrow down
多媒体教学	multimedia teaching
通识教育	general education
多才多艺的；面面俱到的	well-rounded
自律，自我约束	self-discipline
校园暴力	campus violence
吸毒	take drugs
职业准备	career preparation
师生比例	student-faculty ratio
给学生分班	stream pupils
住宿生	boarding student
青少年犯罪	juvenile delinquency
平均绩点	Grade Point Average (GPA)

练习 1 根据下面的中文释义，写出对应的单词（词组）。

A		B	
眼界 h_____		能力 c_____	
多才多艺的 v_____		勤奋的 d_____	
假设 h_____		努力 e_____	
互动 i_____		偏见 b_____	
论文 t_____		住宿生 b_____	
好奇心 c_____		明辨是非 d_____	
死记硬背 r_____		监督 s_____	
有天赋的 g_____		严格的 r_____	
生动的 v_____		学期 t_____	
复习功课 r_____		导师 m_____	
压倒 o_____		小学 p_____	

练习 2 用方框中所给单词（词组）的适当形式填空。

obedience	appeal	proficient	discriminate	indulge in
stifle	diploma	provoke	revise	go astray
deliberate	acute	ignore	undertake	generalist

1. The content of the book is exciting and a_____（吸引）to many students to buy.

2. He finished his study in advance and got his d_____（毕业证书）successfully.

3. Now many schools have i_____（忽视）the moral education of the students.

4. The present education pays attention to cultivate of g_____（全才）.

5. Via this test, students have learnt true o_____（服从）and deference.

6. The professor is p_____（精通的）in English and model painting.

7. He i_____（沉溺于）this problem so that he hadn't slept for three days.

8. He had g_____（误入歧途）when young, and after going to college, he was aware of the importance of learning.

9. This complex mathematical problem has p_____（引起）fierce debate among teachers.

10. I can't u_____（保证）to finish this book, but I will do my best.

11. An educator should not d_____（歧视）against any student because of the physical defects.

12. Faced with such an a_____（严重的）problem, he wanted to pretend nothing happened.

13. To avoid error, she made each decision in d_____（深思熟虑的）.

14. Exam-oriented education will s_____（扼杀）the imagination of children.

15. We need to r_____（修改）the content of our textbook about the linguistics part.

☐ curiosity	☐ outline	☐ acquaint
☐ appeal	☐ generalist	☐ indulge
☐ assignment	☐ specialist	☐ bully
☐ parenting	☐ discipline	☐ enlighten
☐ moral	☐ curriculum	☐ astray
☐ prime	☐ vocational	☐ alienated
☐ tuition	☐ dull	☐ seminar
☐ peer	☐ depend	☐ stomach
☐ elite	☐ obedience	☐ cultivate
☐ deviate	☐ pride	☐ instill
☐ rear	☐ qualified	☐ impart
☐ humanities	☐ rewarding	☐ mold
☐ diploma	☐ schooling	☐ mentor
☐ scholarship	☐ syllabus	☐ counselor
☐ adolescent	☐ vigor	☐ guardian
☐ feedback	☐ unify	☐ academic
☐ teamwork	☐ proficient	☐ comprehensive
☐ ignore	☐ master	☐ enrich
☐ mimic	☐ mature	☐ provoke
☐ pedagogical	☐ critical	☐ docile
☐ adversity	☐ open-minded	☐ perplex
☐ mental	☐ credit	☐ overwhelm
☐ attend	☐ lecture	☐ nerd

☐ diversity	☐ practice	☐ linguistic
☐ insightful	☐ intelligence	☐ gifted
☐ undertake	☐ internship	☐ deliberate
☐ obligation	☐ figure	☐ characteristic
☐ compulsory	☐ interaction	☐ internal
☐ adaptive	☐ capable	☐ persistence
☐ horizon	☐ verbal	☐ stifle
☐ realize	☐ context	☐ creativity
☐ authority	☐ core	☐ theoretical
☐ discriminate	☐ hypothesis	☐ psychological
☐ versatile	☐ obscure	☐ thesis
☐ integration	☐ interest	☐ bibliography
☐ sense	☐ vivid	☐ patriotism
☐ competence	☐ accessibility	☐ foster
☐ acute	☐ expertise	☐ motivation
☐ diligent	☐ acquisitive	☐ literacy
☐ contribution	☐ term	☐ controversial
☐ rote	☐ rigorous	☐ revise
☐ bias	☐ implication	☐ scope
☐ gap	☐ abandon	☐ supervise
☐ endeavor	☐ behave	
☐ distract	☐ optimist	

表中共有 133 个单词

您不确认的单词 _____ 个，占总数的 _____%

如果比例高于 10%，请耐心再复习一遍。如果比例低于 10%，您可以开始下一章的托福写作之旅了！

第二章

工作与成功

income ['ɪnkʌm]

释义· *n.* 收入；所得

例句· 泰德通过晚上打零工来增加收入。

Ted supplemented his income by doing part-time work in the evenings.

搭配· 所得税 income tax

收入差距 income gap

总收入 gross income

lucrative ['luːkrətɪv]

释义· *adj.* 获利多的；赚大钱的

例句· 他主动放弃了可观的酬金，觉得自己的健康更加重要。

He has forfeited a lucrative fee but feels his well-being is more important.

搭配· 肥差 lucrative job

announce [ə'naʊns]

释义· *v.* 宣布；声称；广播

例句· 他将于今晚宣布辞职。

He will announce tonight that he is resigning from office.

派生· announcement *n.* 公告；宣告；发表

搭配· 向某人宣布某事 announce sth. to sb.

setback ['setbæk]

释义· *n.* 挫折；阻碍

例句· 不要让外界的一次失误或挫折影响你，抹杀所有你已经取得的
进步。

Don't allow one slipup, or setback from the outside,
influence you to erase all the progress you've made.

merit ['merɪt]

释义· *n.* 优点；功绩

例句· 今晚的会议将权衡两位候选人的比较优势。

Tonight's meeting will weigh up the relative merits of the
two candidates.

反义· demerit *n.* 缺点；过失

搭配· 根据事物本身的优缺点；按照事情的是非曲直 on its merits

campaign [kæm'peɪn]

释义· *n.* 活动；运动；战役 *vi.* 参加运动；领导运动

例句· 雅拍体育用品公司开展了加强员工培训的活动。

Apacs has launched a campaign to improve the training of
staff.

搭配· 开展活动 launch a campaign

开展反对某人 / 某事的运动 campaign against sb./sth.

reputation [ˌrepjuˈteɪʃn]

释义· *n.* 名声；声望

例句· 她在之前的工作岗位上是出了名的勤奋。

In her last job she gained a reputation as a hard worker.

搭配· 以……闻名　reputation for

有名望的　of reputation

overlook [ˌoʊvərˈlʊk]

释义· *vt.* 忽略；俯瞰

例句· 要想成功，就不能忽略任何一个细节。

If you want to succeed, do not overlook each detail.

搭配· 从……俯瞰　overlook from

invest [ɪnˈvest]

释义· *v.* 投入；授予

例句· 这里的每个人都对自己的事业投入了很多。

Everyone here has invested a lot in their careers.

派生· investment *n.* 投资；投入

investor *n.* 投资者

搭配· 把某物投入某事　invest sth. in sth.

把某物授予某人　invest sb. with sth.

sacrifice [ˈsækrɪfaɪs]

释义· *v.* 牺牲；奉献 *n.* 牺牲；祭品

例句· 为了成功，他牺牲了陪伴自己家人和朋友的时间。

To succeed, he sacrificed his time with his family and friends.

搭配· 以牺牲……为代价　at the sacrifice of

为某人／某事牺牲某物　sacrifice sth. for sb./sth.

occupation [ˌɑːkjuˈpeɪʃn]

释义· *n.* 职业；占有；消遣

例句· 将我们生命中的激情与职业相匹配是很有力量的，它可以显著地提升我们的才能和潜力。

Matching our passions in life with an occupation is powerful, and can promote our talents and potential in significant ways.

同根· occupied *adj.* 使用中的；被占领的

occupational *adj.* 职业的

搭配· 从事某职业 take up an occupation

despair [dɪˈspeɪ]

释义· *vi.* 绝望；丧失信心 *n.* (U) 绝望

例句· 人生教会我们即使是在最困难的时候都不要绝望，因为黑暗之后终将是黎明。

Life teaches us not to despair even in the darkest hour, because after every night there is a day.

派生· despairing *adj.* 令人绝望的

搭配· 对某人 / 某事绝望 despair of sb./sth.

在绝望中 in despair

让某人感到担忧 be the despair of sb.

令某人感到绝望的是 to the despair of sb.

demanding [dɪˈmændɪŋ]

释义· *adj.* 要求高的；苛刻的

例句· 一份高要求的工作往往也是一份高薪的工作。

A demanding job is always a high-paying job as well.

annual ['ænjuəl]

释义· *adj.* 年度的；每年的 *n.* 年刊

例句· 在年会上，股东会聚集起来，选出董事会来管理公司。

At the annual meeting, the shareholders collect and elect a board which then is in charge of the company.

搭配· 年收入 an annual income

年假 annual leave

redundancy [rɪ'dʌndənsi]

释义· *n.* 裁员；解雇；冗余

例句· 数千名银行职员面临裁员，因为他们的雇主要削减成本。

Thousands of bank employees are facing redundancy as their employers cut costs.

同根· redundant *adj.* 多余的；过剩的；被裁减的

eminent ['emɪnənt]

释义· *adj.* 杰出的；著名的；显赫的

例句· 要成为一名杰出的医生，必须掌握大量的知识和技能。

To be an eminent doctor, one must master a lot of knowledge and skills.

派生· eminence *n.* 卓越；显赫

candidate ['kændɪdət]

释义· *n.* 候选人；应试者

例句· 这名候选人与众不同，给面试官留下了很好的印象。

This candidate differed from the others, leaving a good impression for interviewers.

搭配· ……的候选人 a candidate for sth.

appointment [ə'pɔɪntmənt]

释义· *n.* 任命；委任；约定；职位

例句· 关于他的任命尚未正式宣布，消息就已经泄露了出去。

The news of his appointment filtered out before it was officially advertised.

搭配· 与某人约定 make an appointment with sb.

面谈预约 interview appointment

workshop ['wɜːrkʃɑːp]

释义· *n.* 工作室；车间；研讨会；研习班

例句· 在成名前，她在艾奥瓦作家工作室学习写作。

She studied writing at the Iowa Writers Workshop before becoming famous.

rival ['raɪvl]

释义· *adj.* 竞争的 *n.* 对手；竞争者 *v.* 与……相匹敌

例句· 希娜辞了职，转投一家对手公司工作。

Sheena left her job and went to work for a rival company.

派生· rivalry *n.* 竞争；对抗

rivalrous *adj.* 敌对性的；有竞争性的

搭配· 竞争对手公司 a rival company

effective [ɪ'fektɪv]

释义· *adj.* 有效的；起作用的；实际的

例句· 为了更有效地完成任务，你的团队应该一次只执行一个任务。

To be effective, your group should pursue only one objective at a time.

反义· ineffective *adj.* 无效的；不起作用的

stability [stə'bɪləti]

释义· *n.* (U) 稳定性；坚定

例句· 许多求职者看重的是工作的稳定性，而不是高薪。

Many candidates value the stability of the job, but not the high salary.

同根· stabilize *v.* （使）稳定

leadership ['liːdərʃɪp]

释义· *n.* (U) 领导；领导阶层

例句· 最有才干的领导也会陷于拘泥琐事的困境中。

The most brilliant leadership can be mired in detail.

搭配· 在某人的领导下　under sb.'s leadership

领导的素质 / 技巧　leadership qualities/skills

personnel [ˌpɜːrsə'nel]

释义· *n.* (pl.) 全体人员；职员

例句· 工厂所有管理人员都是聘用的。

All the managerial personnel at the factory are hired on contract.

同义· staff *n.* 全体职工；职员

搭配· 人员培训　personnel training

dismiss [dɪs'mɪs]

释义· *v.* 解雇；开除；不予理会；解散

例句· 员工可能会因为发送粗俗的电子邮件而被解雇。

Employees can be dismissed for sending obscene emails.

派生· dismissal *n.* 解雇；免职

搭配· 从……解雇某人　dismiss sb. from sth.

因某事而解雇某人　dismiss sb. for sth.

prestige [preˈstiːʒ]

释义 · *n.* (U) 威望；声望 *adj.* 令人敬仰的；受尊重的

例句 · 这家名不见经传的英国公司如今已经声名鹊起。

This little-known British firm has now gained considerable prestige.

blunder [ˈblʌndər]

释义 · *n.* 大错；愚蠢的错误 *v.* 犯愚蠢的错误；误入

例句 · 我犯了个大错，然后我告诉自己绝不会再重蹈覆辙。

I made a blunder, and I tell myself that I'll never make that mistake again.

派生 · blundering *adj.* 浮躁的；愚笨的

搭配 · 无意中陷入（困境）blunder into/in sth.

抛弃；错失 blunder away

concession [kənˈseʃn]

释义 · *n.* 让步；承认；特许权

例句 · 成功者知道什么时候该做出让步，什么时候该坚持立场。

Winners know when to make concessions and when to take a stand.

搭配 · 对某人的让步 a concession to sb.

在某事上的让步 a concession on sth.

affiliate [əˈfɪliət]

释义 · *n.* 分支机构；分公司；附属机构

例句 · 这家跨国公司在大约 120 个国家内设有分支机构。

This multinational corporation has affiliates in around 120 countries.

派生 · affiliated *adj.* 隶属的；附属的

solidarity [ˌsɑːlɪ'dærəti]

释义· *n.* (U) 团结；一致

例句· 这家新公司把成功归功于团结：每个人都像是这个大家庭中的一员。

The new company owes its success to the solidarity: everyone is like a member of a big family.

同根· solidify *v.* （使）凝固；（使）变稳固

solidification *n.* 凝固

glorious ['glɔːriəs]

释义· *adj.* 辉煌的；光荣的；壮丽的

例句· 许多人只关注她辉煌的成就，而忽视她艰辛的努力。

Many people only focus on her glorious achievements but ignore her hard work.

搭配· 光荣革命 Glorious Revolution

encourage [ɪn'kɜːrɪdʒ]

释义· *vt.* 鼓励；激励；支持

例句· 这就是为什么大家都在思索，如何才能培养企业家精神，如何鼓励创新。

That's why many of them are thinking really very hard on how to foster entrepreneurship, how to encourage innovation.

派生· encouragement *n.* 鼓励

encouraging *adj.* 令人鼓舞的；振奋人心的

搭配· 鼓励某人做某事 encourage sb. to do sth.

career [kə'rɪr]

释义· *n.* 事业；生涯；职业

例句· 最大的快乐莫过于事业上的成功。
There's no greater happiness than that of succeeding in one's career.

搭配· 生涯规划 career planning
学历；学业 academic career
职业阶梯 career ladder
向上爬；谋求发迹 make a career
招聘会 career fair

painstaking ['peɪnzteɪkɪŋ]

释义· *adj.* 极其仔细的；十分小心的；缜密的

例句· 这项工作被一丝不苟地完成了。
The work had been done with painstaking attention to detail.

搭配· 心血；辛苦的努力 painstaking effort

relentless [rɪ'lentləs]

释义· *adj.* 坚韧的；不屈不挠的；不间断的

例句· 对质量孜孜不倦的追求使他的技能出类拔萃。
Relentless in his pursuit of quality, his technical ability was remarkable.

aptitude ['æptɪtuːd]

释义· *n.* 天资；天赋；才能

例句· 他善于和儿童打交道的本事使他得到了这份工作。
His aptitude for dealing with children got him the job.

搭配· 做某事的才能 aptitude for doing sth.

salary ['sæləri]

释义· *n.* 工资；薪水

例句· 她换了一份工资更高的工作。

She moved to a job with a higher salary.

搭配· 基本薪金 basic salary

月薪　monthly salary

年薪　annual salary

可观的薪水　handsome salary

> **扩展** 三种"薪水"的区别：
>
> salary 指办公室工作人员、教师、医生等专业人员按月领取的薪金。
>
> wages 指在工厂等工作的雇员按周领取的工钱。
>
> pay 指工资或薪水。

industrious [ɪn'dʌstriəs]

释义· *adj.* 勤奋的；勤劳的

例句· 第一，没有任何成就是可以在短时间内达到的，都需要持续的勤奋工作和努力。

Firstly, no accomplishment can be achieved in a short time, and success asks for continuous industrious work and efforts.

同根· industrial *adj.* 工业的

promotion [prə'moʊʃn]

释义· *n.* 晋升；提升；促销活动

例句· 我想要一份有良好晋升机会的工作。

I want a job with good prospects for promotion.

搭配· 促销；促销活动　sales promotion

status ['steɪtəs]

释义· *n.* 地位；身份

例句· 医生历来都享有很高的社会地位。

Doctors have traditionally enjoyed a high social status.

搭配· 现状 status quo

地位低下 / 高的工作 high/low status jobs

collective [kə'lektɪv]

释义· *n.* 集团；集合体 *adj.* 集体的；共同的

例句· 这伙人是一个集体，做每件事情都在一起，至少分钱时是这样。

The gang was a collective, and either did everything together or, at least, shared the profits.

同根· collectivism *n.* 集体主义

exert [ɪg'zɜːrt]

释义· *vt.* 努力；运用；行使；施加

例句· 他必须努力才能成功。

In order to be successful he would have to exert himself.

派生· exertion *n.* 发挥；运用；努力

搭配· 努力；尽力 exert oneself

对……产生影响 exert an influence on

tenacity [tə'næsəti]

释义· *n.* (U) 坚韧；坚毅

例句· 事业要成功，才能、勤奋和顽强的意志都至关重要。

Talent, hard work and sheer tenacity are all crucial to career success.

同根· tenacious *adj.* 顽强的；固执的；坚韧的

colleague ['kɑːliːg]

释义· *n.* 同事；同僚

例句· 在没有和同事商量的情况下，他从洛杉矶飞到了芝加哥。

Without consulting his colleagues, he flew from Los Angeles

to Chicago.

派生· colleagueship *n.* 共事；同事关系

imprudent [ɪm'pruːdnt]

释义· *adj.* 轻率的；不谨慎的

例句· 汤姆为这个轻率的行为付出了代价，他被老板开除了。

Tom paid the price for his imprudent behavior: he was fired by his boss.

反义· prudent *adj.* 谨慎的；精明的

overwork [ˌoʊvər'wɜːrk]

释义· *v.* （使）过度工作；（使）过度劳累

例句· 他工作太累，而且非常操心。

He's overworking and has got a lot on his mind.

passionate ['pæʃənət]

释义· *adj.* 热情的；狂热的

例句· 我仅仅是简单地用我对这份工作的热情和热爱在追逐目标。

I simply pursued it because I was passionate about it and loved the work.

反义· passionless *adj.* 不热情的；冷淡的

fervent ['fɜːrvənt]

释义· *adj.* 热情的；热烈的

例句· 他对成功有种强烈的热情，甚至不惜一切代价。

He has a fervent passion for success, even at all costs.

recruitment [rɪ'kruːtmənt]

释义· *n.* (U) 招聘

例句· 这家公司的招聘要求非常严格，很少有人能通过面试。

The company has stringent recruitment requirements, and few people can pass the interview.

搭配· 人员招聘 personnel recruitment

measure [ˈmeʒər]

释义· *n.* 衡量；措施；办法 *v.* 衡量；测量

例句· 收入是衡量一个人成功与否的重要标准，但不是唯一标准。
Income is an important measure of a person's success, but not the only criterion.

派生· measurement *n.* 测量

搭配· 是……的评判标准；是……的体现 be a measure of sth.
（不彻底的）折中办法 half measures
将……与……作比较 measure sb./sth. against sb./sth.

strive [straɪv]

释义· *vi.* 努力；奋斗

例句· 我们的使命要求我们在所有工作中都要更加努力拼搏。
Our mission demands that we shall always strive for more, in all that we do.

搭配· 努力做某事 strive to do sth.
争取某物 strive for sth.
反抗某事 strive against sth.

扩展· strove (过去式) striven (过去分词)

assiduous [əˈsɪdʒuəs]

释义· *adj.* 刻苦的；勤勉的

例句· 他刻苦钻研的精神值得效法。
His spirit of assiduous study is worthy of emulation.

同根· assiduity *n.* 勤勉；刻苦

insomnia [ɪn'sɑːmniə]

释义· *n.* (U) 失眠；失眠症

例句· 任何工作的压力都会引起头痛、失眠、皮肤问题、暴饮暴食或者食欲不振。

Stress at any job can lead to headaches, insomnia, skin problems, overeating or loss of appetite.

negotiate [nɪ'ɡoʊʃieɪt]

释义· *v.* 谈判；协商；通过

例句· 因为在一些细节上有分歧，这家公司与客户的谈判失败了。

The company failed to negotiate with its customers because of differences in details.

派生· negotiation *n.* 谈判；转让

搭配· （为某事）与某人谈判　negotiate with sb. (for/about sth.)

administration [əd,mɪnɪ'streɪʃn]

释义· *n.* （企业、学校等的）管理；行政

例句· 这家公司正在寻找一个有管理经验的人。

This firm is looking for someone with experience in administration.

同根· administrate *vt.* 管理；经营

administrative *adj.* 管理的；行政的

customer ['kʌstəmər]

释义· *n.* 客户；顾客

例句· 我们力求为所有的客户提供物有所值的商品和服务。

We aim to offer good value and service to all our customers.

搭配· 客户服务；售后服务　customer service

客户至上；顾客至上　customer first

brand [brænd]

释义· *n.* 品牌；牌子；烙印 *v.* 给……打上烙印

例句· 这家公司通过十年的时间建立了自己的品牌，却在一夕之间摧毁
了它。

This company established its brand in ten years but destroyed
it within one day.

搭配· 把某人归为某类（往往是不好的）brand sb. (as) sth.

品牌形象 brand image

全新的；崭新的 brand new

feasible ['fi:zəbl]

释义· *adj.* 可行的；可能的

例句· 公司的董事会最终投票认为这是一个可行的方案。

The company's board of directors eventually voted that this
was a feasible option.

派生· feasibility *n.* 可行性；可能性

enthusiastic [ɪn,θu:zi'æstɪk]

释义· *adj.* 热情的；热心的

例句· 她对这份工作非常地热情，很快就得到了老板的赏识。

She was very enthusiastic about the job and was soon
appreciated by her boss.

搭配· 对（做）某事很有热情 be enthusiastic about (doing) sth.

发烧友 enthusiastic fan

profile ['prəʊfaɪl]

释义· *n.* 人物简介；侧面；轮廓 *v.* 扼要介绍

例句· 由他的个人资料我们可以断定他以前是个成功的商人。

From his profile, we can conclude that he was a successful

businessman before.

搭配· 引人注目　a high profile

保持低调　keep a low profile

提升某人的形象　raise sb.'s profile

shift [ʃɪft]

释义· *n.* 班；轮班；移动；改变 *v.* 转移；改变

例句· 戴夫昨天不得不上一个 12 小时的班。

Dave had to work a 12-hour shift yesterday.

搭配· 夜班　night shift

轮班作业　shift work

把……移走　shift away

推卸责任（给某人）shift the blame/responsibility (onto sb.)

determine [dɪ'tɜ:rmɪn]

释义· *v.* 决心；决定

例句· 上次他失败了，所以这次他决心不重蹈覆辙。

Last time he failed, so he was determined that the same mistakes would not be repeated this time.

搭配· 决定做某事　determine to do sth.

peculiar [pɪ'kju:liər]

释义· *adj.* 独特的；特殊的；奇怪的

例句· 他有自己独特的风格，你很快就会习惯的。

He has his own peculiar style which you'll soon get used to.

搭配· 为某人 / 某物所特有　be peculiar to sb./sth.

stubborn ['stʌbərn]

释义· *adj.* 固执的；顽强的；难处理的

例句· 成功者往往都非常固执，不达目的不罢休。

Successful people are always very stubborn and don't stop until they reach their goal.

派生· stubbornness *n.* 倔强；顽强

搭配· 顽疾 stubborn ills

事实是不可否认的 facts are stubborn things

bargain ['bɑːrgən]

释义· *v.* 讨价还价；商谈 *n.* 交易；便宜货

例句· 不要和你的领导讨价还价，做好自己的本职工作，不要担心领导不会赏识你。

Don't bargain with your leader, do your job and don't worry that the leader won't appreciate you.

搭配· 与某人讨价还价 bargain with sb.

预料到某事 bargain for/on sth.

另外；而且；也 into the bargain

aspiring [ə'spaɪərɪŋ]

释义· *adj.* 有抱负的；有志向的

例句· 在短短两页纸内，有抱负的企业家必须让投资者们相信他们的诚恳以及计划的合理性。

In no more than two pages, aspiring entrepreneurs must convince investors with their integrity, as well as the plausibility of their plan.

同根· aspiration *n.* 渴望；抱负

cooperate [koʊ'ɑːpəreɪt]

释义· *vi.* 合作；配合

例句· 我们能否成功取决于我们合作的好坏。

Whether we can succeed depends on how well we

cooperate.

派生· cooperative *adj.* 合作的

cooperation *n.* 合作

搭配· 与某人合作 cooperate with sb.

resolve [rɪ'zɑːlv]

释义· *n.* (U) 决心 *v.* 作出决定；解决

例句· 成功者往往会把思想上升为决心和行动。

Winners often make the thinking ripen into resolve and action.

派生· resolved *adj.* 下决心的

搭配· 决心做某事 resolve to do sth.

（使 A）分解为 B；（A）逐步变成 B resolve (sth.) into sth.

harmony ['hɑːrməni]

释义· *n.* 和睦；协调；融洽；和声

例句· 新来的这位员工和其他人都相处得非常和睦，无论是上级还是同事。

The new employee is in harmony with other people from superiors to colleagues.

派生· harmonious *adj.* 和谐的；和睦的

搭配· 与某物一致；与某物协调 be in harmony with sth.

和谐无间 in harmony

workload ['wɜːrkloʊd]

释义· *n.* 工作量

例句· 我们必须想办法减少盖尔明年的工作量。

We've got to find ways of reducing Gail's workload next year.

asset ['æset]

释义 · *n.* 财富；资产；财产

例句 · 她的领导才能是保守党最宝贵的财富。

Her leadership qualities were the greatest asset of the Conservative Party.

搭配 · 对于某人 / 某物来说是一份财富 be an asset to sb./sth.

无形的资产 intangible asset

earnings ['ɜːrnɪŋz]

释义 · *n.* (*pl.*) 收入；所赚的钱

例句 · 他对自己会计师的收入很满意。

He was satisfied with his earnings as an accountant.

collaborate [kə'læbəreɪt]

释义 · *vi.* 合作；协作；通敌

例句 · 如果你想把那些重要的、持久的、有意义的事情做好，你必须合作。

If you want to get things done, for those critical, enduring, meaningful things, you have to collaborate.

派生 · collaborative *adj.* 合作的

collaboration *n.* 合作

搭配 · 在某事上与某人合作 collaborate with sb. on sth.

与某人合作（做）某事 collaborate with sb. in (doing) sth.

résumé ['rezəmeɪ]

释义 · *n.* 简历

例句 · 寄出你的简历并附上一份针对那个特定工作岗位的求职信。

Send your résumé with a cover letter that is specific to that particular job.

搭配· personal résumé 个人简历

> **扩展**　两种简历的区别：
>
> résumé 较短，一般就一页纸，主要是突出自己的工作经验和工作技能。
>
> curriculum vitae（CV）内容比较多，在美国主要用于申请学术、教育、科研职位，或者申请奖学金等。

morale [mə'ræl]

释义· *n.* (U) 士气；斗志

例句· 一个好的领导必须知道开怀大笑能帮助你建立和谐关系、鼓舞士气、缓解工作压力下的紧张情绪。

A good leader must know that a good laugh can help you build rapport, boost morale, and deflate tension when working under stressful situations.

搭配· 员工士气　staff/employee morale

鼓舞 / 提高士气 / 增强信心　boost/raise/improve morale

agency ['eɪdʒənsi]

释义· *n.* 代理处；经销处

例句· 他通过一个职业介绍所得到这份工作。

He got the job through an employment agency.

搭配· 在某人 / 某物的帮助下　through the agency of sb./sth.

通讯社　news agency

旅行社　travel agency

decisiveness [dɪ'saɪsɪvnəs]

释义· *n.* (U) 果断；决断力

例句· 一旦你找到了合适的人才，速度和果断就是关键。

Once you find the right candidate, speed and decisiveness

are key.

同根· decisive *adj.* 决定性的；果断的

embrace [ɪmˈbreɪs]

释义· *v.* 欣然接受，乐意采纳（思想、建议等）；拥抱 *n.* 拥抱

例句· 他迎接新的信息时代的到来。

He embraces the new information age.

persevere [ˌpɜːrsəˈvɪr]

释义· *vi.* 坚持不懈；锲而不舍

例句· 如果你坚持找工作，最后，你肯定会找到合适的工作。

If you persevere in your search for a job, you are sure to find something suitable in the end.

派生· perseverance *n.* 毅力；韧性；不屈不挠的精神

搭配· 坚持（做）某事 persevere in (doing) sth.

锲而不舍地帮助某人 persevere with sb.

adept [əˈdept]

释义· *adj.* 擅长的；熟练的；内行的

例句· 他们还需要擅长与信息技术部门之外的同事合作。

They also need to be adept at collaborating with colleagues outside of IT.

派生· adeptness *n.* 熟练

搭配· 擅长（做）某事 be adept at/in (doing) sth.

compatible [kəmˈpætəbl]

释义· *adj.* 兼容的；能共处的

例句· 他的性格和这份工作不符，最后只能辞职了。

His character is not compatible with the job, so he has to resign at last.

搭配· 与……和谐相处；与……相配的 be compatible with

staff [stæf]

释义· *n.* 职员；全体职工；棍棒

例句· 今年全体员工工作都非常出色。

The entire staff has done an outstanding job this year.

派生· staffing *n.* 人员配置

inexperienced [ˌɪnɪkˈspɪriənst]

释义· *adj.* 缺乏经验的

例句· 当然，与经验丰富的员工相比，新手需要给予更多的关注与指导。

New or inexperienced employees naturally require more attention and handholding than those who are seasoned at their jobs.

devoted [dɪˈvoʊtɪd]

释义· *adj.* 致力（于……）的；热衷的；挚爱的

例句· 他从事这项工作已有十多年了，取得了显著的成就。

He was devoted to this job for over ten years and made remarkable achievements.

同根· devotion *n.* 献身；忠诚

搭配· 致力（于……）的 be devoted to

certification [ˌsɜːrtɪfɪˈkeɪʃn]

释义· *n.* 证书；证明

例句· 这种证书将帮助他们得到晋升。

This certification will aid them in their promotion.

同根· certificate *n.* 证明；结业证书

certified *adj.* 有资质的；有保证的

ambitious [æm'bɪʃəs]

释义 · *adj.* 有野心的；有抱负的；雄心勃勃的

例句 · 这位野心勃勃的年轻人利用朋友往上爬。

The ambitious young man used his friends to further his career.

employ [ɪm'plɔɪ]

释义 · *v.* 雇用；使用；采用

例句 · 这家工厂雇用了 2000 多名员工。

The factory employs over 2,000 people.

搭配 · 从事于；忙于做某事 be employed in doing sth.

替某人工作；为某人所雇用 in sb.'s employ/in the employ of sb.

incline [ɪn'klaɪn]

释义 · *v.* （使）倾向于；有……的趋势

例句 · 这次意外使他重新考虑他的职业。

The accident inclined him to reconsider his career.

派生 · inclination *n.* 倾向；爱好

搭配 · 倾向于做某事 incline to do sth.

consensus [kən'sensəs]

释义 · *n.* 一致的意见；共识

例句 · 委员会对收购另外一家公司达成了一致意见。

The committee reached a consensus on the acquisition of another company.

搭配 · 达成共识 reach a consensus

motto ['mɑːtoʊ]

释义· *n.* 座右铭；格言

例句· 谦卑是他的人生座右铭，正因如此，他一直在工作上保持低调，最后一鸣惊人。

Humility is his life's motto, that's why he kept a low profile at work and finally made a great coup.

搭配· 校训　school motto

扩展· mottoes/mottos (*pl.*)

profession [prəˈfeʃn]

释义· *n.* （需要高等教育或训练的）职业，行业；宣布；表白

例句· 他妒忌她在她的职业中已取得的地位。

He envies her the position she has achieved in her profession.

派生· professional *adj.* 专业的；职业的

fierce [fɪrs]

释义· *adj.* 激烈的；凶猛的

例句· 争夺斯柯达股份的竞争极为激烈。

Competition has been fierce to win a stake in Skoda.

搭配· 激烈的竞争　fierce competition

convince [kənˈvɪns]

释义· *v.* 使确信；使信服；说服

例句· 他使我确信这件工作的艰巨性。

He convinced me of the difficulty of the work.

同义· persuade *v.* 使信服；使相信

搭配· 使某人确信某物　convince sb. of sth.

说服某人做某事　convince sb. to do sth.

resign [rɪ'zaɪn]

释义· *v.* 辞职；顺从

例句· 上周她辞去了政府部门的工作。

She resigned from the government last week.

搭配· 从……辞职 resign from

使自己顺从于（做）某事 resign yourself to (doing) sth.

prosper ['prɑːspər]

释义· *v.* 兴旺；繁荣；发达；成功

例句· 自从他的生意兴隆以来，他们一直过着优裕的生活。

They have been living on easy street since his business

began to prosper.

派生· prosperity *n.* 繁荣；成功

prosperous *adj.* 繁荣的；兴旺的

inferior [ɪn'fɪriər]

释义· *adj.* 级别低的；较差的；次的 *n.* 不如别人的人

例句· 他拒绝接受职位低的工作。

He refused to accept a job of inferior status.

派生· inferiority *n.* 低等；劣等

搭配· 在……方面低劣 inferior in

比不上某人 / 某物的 be inferior to sb./sth.

attribute [ə'trɪbjuːt]

释义· *vt.* 把……归因于；认为……是由于

例句· 他把他的成功归因于团队的力量。

He attributed his success to the strength of his team.

派生· attribution *n.* 归因；归属

搭配· 把某事归因于某人 / 某物 attribute sth. to sb./sth.

triumph ['traɪʌmf]

释义· *n.* 胜利；成就 *vi.* 打败；战胜

例句· 在他上任之后，他打败了对手公司，这是一项伟大的个人胜利。

After he took office, he defeated his rival company, which is a great personal triumph.

派生· triumphant *adj.* 成功的；得意洋洋的

搭配· 胜利地；洋洋得意地 in triumph

战胜某人 / 某物 triumph over sb./sth.

endorse [ɪn'dɔːrs]

释义· *vt.* 赞同；支持；背书

例句· 董事会不赞同他的计划，认为太过冒险和激进。

The board didn't endorse his plan, saying it was too risky and radical.

派生· endorsement *n.* 认可；支持

grumble ['grʌmbl]

释义· *v.* 抱怨；发牢骚

例句· 他们抱怨自己的工作很辛苦。

They grumble about how hard their work is.

派生· grumbler *n.* 爱抱怨的人；发牢骚的人

搭配· 对某人 / 某事表示不满 grumble at/about sb./sth.

tough [tʌf]

释义· *adj.* 坚强的；吃苦耐劳的；坚韧不拔的

例句· 他树立了铁面生意人的名声。

He built up a reputation as a tough businessman.

搭配· （表示同情）倒霉，不走运 tough luck

严厉的爱 tough love

扩展· tougher（比较级）toughest（最高级）

crave [kreɪv]

释义· v. 渴望；渴求

例句· 她有雇主们渴望的工作态度和职业道德。

She has the kind of attitude and work ethic that employers crave.

搭配· 渴望某物 crave for sth.

prone [proʊn]

释义· *adj.* 有……倾向的；易于……的；俯卧的

例句· 面对微软和苹果公司的邀请函，他倾向于选择后者。

Faced with invitations from Microsoft and Apple, he was prone to the latter.

搭配· 有做某事的倾向 be prone to do sth.

accumulate [əˈkjuːmjəleɪt]

释义· v. 积累；堆积

例句· 青少年可以在兼职工作中积累社会经验。

Teenagers can accumulate social experience through part-time jobs.

派生· accumulated *adj.* 积累的；累计的

accumulation *n.* 积聚

manage [ˈmænɪdʒ]

释义· v. 管理；设法做到；成功应对

例句· 他被要求去管理一个新的部门。

He was asked to manage a new department.

派生· management *n.* 管理；操纵

manageable *adj.* 易管理的；好办的

搭配· 设法做成某事　manage to do sth.

　　　　用 / 不用某物设法对付　manage with/without sth.

　　　　凑合着活下去　manage on

bankruptcy [ˈbæŋkrʌptsi]

释义· *n.* 破产；倒闭

例句· 泛美航空公司是两个月内第二家申请破产的航空公司。

　　　　Pan Am is the second airline in two months to file for bankruptcy.

同义· insolvency *n.* 破产

flawless [ˈflɔːləs]

释义· *adj.* 完美的；无瑕的

例句· 没有人是完美的，但成功者知道如何规避自己的弱点。

　　　　No one is flawless, but a winner knows how to avoid his or her weakness.

同义· perfect *adj.* 完美的；完全的

strategy [ˈstrætədʒi]

释义· *n.* 战略；策略

例句· 公司首先必须解决战略规划问题。

　　　　The company must first resolve questions of strategy.

同义· tactic *n.* 策略；战术

派生· strategic *adj.* 战略上的

搭配· 做某事的策略　strategy to do/ for doing sth.

luminary [ˈluːmɪneri]

释义· *n.* 名人；杰出的人物；大师

例句· 想成为一个领域里的名人，就必须做出一些革命性的研究。

　　　　To be the luminary in one field, one must conduct some

groundbreaking researches.

派生· luminous *adj.* 发光的；清楚的

arena [ə'ri:nə]

释义· *n.* 舞台；竞技场；活动场所

例句· 这家公司为每一位员工提供了一个公平竞争的舞台。

This company provides an arena for each employee, where they can compete equally.

compensate ['kɑ:mpenseɪt]

释义· *v.* 补偿；赔偿

例句· 公司将对工人的收入损失做出补偿。

The firm will compensate workers for their loss of earnings.

派生· compensation *n.* 补偿物；赔偿金

compensable *adj.* 可补偿的

搭配· 补偿某人某物 compensate sb. for sth.

crew [kru:]

释义· *n.* 全体人员；全体船员

例句· 主管为全体人员举办了一次生日宴会，并激励大家努力工作。

The supervisor held a birthday party for the crew and stimulated everyone to work hard.

搭配· 全体机务人员 crew members

一个电影摄制组 a film crew

coincidence [koʊ'ɪnsɪdəns]

释义· *n.* 巧合；同时存在

例句· 有时候，成功需要运气和巧合。

Sometimes, success needs luck and coincidence.

同根· coincident *adj.* 一致的；符合的；同时发生的

搭配· 碰巧 by coincidence

recognition [ˌrekəɡˈnɪʃn]

释义· *n.* 认可；赞赏；好评

例句· 最后，她父亲的工作得到了大众的认可。

At last, her father's work has received popular recognition.

reap [riːp]

释义· *v.* 获得；收获；收割

例句· 它帮助企业实现其目标，并且获得企业利润。

It helps an enterprise realize its goals and reap business benefits.

搭配· 获得……的益处 reap the benefits of

种瓜得瓜，种豆得豆 you reap what you sow

enterprise [ˈentərpraɪz]

释义· *n.* 企业；事业；进取心；事业心

例句· 这家企业的远景极其美好。

The enterprise has excellent prospects.

派生· enterpriser *n.* 企业家

enterprising *adj.* 有事业心的；有进取心的

dedicated [ˈdedɪkeɪtɪd]

释义· *adj.* 专注的；有奉献精神的

例句· 你不会找到更好的求职者或者更专注的员工了。

You won't find a better candidate or a more dedicated employee.

搭配· 献身于；贡献；致力于 be dedicated to

compromise ['kɑ:prəmaɪz]

释义· v. 妥协；违背（原则） n. 妥协；和解

例句· 要想成功，就不能向困难妥协。

If you want to succeed, you can't compromise with difficulties.

派生· compromising adj. 妥协的；让步的

搭配· 达成妥协 reach a compromise

妥协；做出让步 make a compromise

partner ['pɑ:rtnər]

释义· n. 合伙人；搭档；配偶 v. 结成伙伴

例句· 我和我的合作伙伴最近都失去了我们在城市的工作。

My partner and I have both recently lost our jobs in the City.

派生· partnership n. 合作；合作关系

搭配· 一位贸易伙伴 a trading partner

做某人的伙伴 partner with sb.

reluctant [rɪ'lʌktənt]

释义· adj. 不情愿的；勉强的

例句· 很多人都不情愿做出改变，所以他们始终无法获得成功。

Many people are reluctant to make changes, so they would never be successful.

搭配· 不愿意做某事；勉强做某事 be reluctant to do sth.

charisma [kə'rɪzmə]

释义· n. (U) 个人魅力；感召力

例句· 作为领导，他既没有谋略也没有个人魅力去鼓舞人。

He, as a leader, has neither the strategy nor the personal charisma to inspire people.

派生· charismatic *adj.* 有超凡魅力的；有感召力的

conflict [kən'flɪkt]

释义· *vi.* 冲突；争执
例句· 个人道德与职业道德之间有时会相冲突。
　　　Personal ethics and professional ethics sometimes conflict.
派生· conflicting *adj.* 冲突的；矛盾的
搭配· 与某物冲突 conflict with sth.

zeal [ziːl]

释义· *n.* 热忱；热情
例句· 他以极大的热忱对待这份工作。
　　　He approached the job with missionary zeal.
派生· zealous *adj.* 热心的；热情的
搭配· 对某事很热心 zeal for/in sth.
　　　以极大的热情做某事 in one's zeal to do sth.

evaluation [ɪˌvæljuˈeɪʃn]

释义· *n.* 评估；评价
例句· 在综合评估之后，汤姆决定放弃这份工作，去寻找新的工作。
　　　After the comprehensive evaluation, Tom decided to quit this job and to find a new one.
同根· evaluative *adj.* 评估的；评价的

dogged ['dɔːgɪd]

释义· *adj.* 顽强的；坚持不懈的
例句· 他们凭借顽强的毅力慢慢地为自己的努力赢得了尊重。
　　　They have, through sheer dogged determination, slowly gained respect for their efforts.

formidable ['fɔːrmɪdəbl]

释义· *adj.* 难对付的；令人敬畏的；可怕的

例句· 我们业务的每一方面都面临着强大的竞争。

We face formidable competition in every aspect of our business.

搭配· 艰巨的挑战；巨大的挑战 formidable challenge

workaholic [ˌwɜːrkəˈhɔːlɪk]

释义· *n.* 工作狂；醉心于工作的人

例句· 那时候的我，有点像一个工作狂，一周至少工作 60 个小时。

At the time, I was somewhat of a workaholic, clocking in sixty-hour weeks.

释义	短语
正确看待……	put...into perspective
（个人、社会群体、阶层）向更高层社会的流动	upward mobility
人才流动	flow of personnel
磨难	trials and tribulations
家喻户晓的名字	a household name
行为准则	code of conduct
深思熟虑的	well-thought-out
名利	fame and fortune
竞争激烈的（世界）	dog-eat-dog
对……印象很深	be deeply impressed with
向往	yearn/long for
昙花一现	be a flash in the pan
一份体面的工作	a decent job
一夜成名的人	overnight celebrity
达到某人的目标	attain one's goal
收入颇丰	a fat salary
白领／蓝领	white-collar/blue-collar worker

建立功勋	accomplish a feat
找到用武之地	find one's niche
发挥自己的潜能	fulfill one's potential
非常难做的工作	back-breaking work
平衡工作与生活	balance work and life
高薪工作	high-paying job
迎接挑战	rise to the challenge
目标远大	aim high
转折点	turning point
人际关系	interpersonal relationship
职业道德	work ethic
心理压力	psychological strain
长期目标	long-term goal
致力于做某事	be committed to doing sth.
尽最大努力（做）	stretch oneself (to do)
以身作则	lead by example
临时工	temporary worker
兼职	part-time job
千方百计；尽一切努力	leave no stone unturned

巩固练习

练习1　根据下面的中文释义，写出对应的单词（词组）。

A

坚持不懈 p_____

天资 a_____

兴旺 p_____

积累 a_____

兼容的 c_____

士气 m_____

人际关系 i_____

向往 y_____

把……归因于 a_____

要求高的 d_____

年度的 a_____

B

高薪工作 h_____

蓝领 b_____

补偿 c_____

有野心的 a_____

职业道德 w_____

赞同 e_____

名声 r_____

破产 b_____

战略 s_____

一份体面的工作 a_____

决心 d_____

练习2　用方框中所给单词（词组）的适当形式填空。

dismiss	bargain with	painstaking	exert	resign from
enthusiastic	announce	strive for	sacrifice	endorse
adept at	eminent	resolve	workaholic	convince

1. He will a_____ (宣布) tonight that he is resigning from office.

2. To succeed, he s_____ (牺牲) his time with his family and friends.

3. To be an e_____ (杰出的) doctor, one must master a lot of

knowledge and skills.

4. Employees can be d_____ (解雇) for sending obscene emails.

5. The work had been done with p_____ (极其仔细的) attention to detail.

6. In order to be successful he would have to e_____ (努力) himself.

7. Our mission demands that we shall always s_____ (奋斗) more, in all that we do.

8. She was very e_____ (热情的) about the job and was soon appreciated by her boss.

9. Don't b_____ (讨价还价) your leader, do your job and don't worry that the leader won't appreciate you.

10. Winners often make the thinking ripen into r_____ (决心) and action.

11. They also need to be a_____ (擅长) collaborating with colleagues outside of IT.

12. He c_____ (使确信) me of the difficulty of the work.

13. She r_____ (辞职) the government last week.

14. The board didn't e_____ (赞同) his plan, saying it was too risky and radical.

15. At the time, I was somewhat of a w_____ (工作狂), clocking in sixty-hour weeks.

☐ income	☐ dismiss	☐ recruitment
☐ lucrative	☐ prestige	☐ measure
☐ announce	☐ blunder	☐ strive
☐ setback	☐ concession	☐ assiduous
☐ merit	☐ affiliate	☐ insomnia
☐ campaign	☐ solidarity	☐ negotiate
☐ reputation	☐ glorious	☐ administration
☐ overlook	☐ encourage	☐ customer
☐ invest	☐ career	☐ brand
☐ sacrifice	☐ painstaking	☐ feasible
☐ occupation	☐ relentless	☐ enthusiastic
☐ despair	☐ aptitude	☐ profile
☐ demanding	☐ salary	☐ shift
☐ annual	☐ industrious	☐ determine
☐ redundancy	☐ promotion	☐ peculiar
☐ eminent	☐ status	☐ stubborn
☐ candidate	☐ collective	☐ bargain
☐ appointment	☐ exert	☐ aspiring
☐ workshop	☐ tenacity	☐ cooperate
☐ rival	☐ colleague	☐ resolve
☐ effective	☐ imprudent	☐ harmony
☐ stability	☐ overwork	☐ workload
☐ leadership	☐ passionate	☐ asset
☐ personnel	☐ fervent	☐ earnings

☐ collaborate	☐ convince	☐ coincidence
☐ résumé	☐ resign	☐ recognition
☐ morale	☐ prosper	☐ reap
☐ agency	☐ inferior	☐ enterprise
☐ decisiveness	☐ attribute	☐ dedicated
☐ embrace	☐ triumph	☐ compromise
☐ persevere	☐ endorse	☐ partner
☐ adept	☐ grumble	☐ reluctant
☐ compatible	☐ tough	☐ charisma
☐ staff	☐ crave	☐ conflict
☐ inexperienced	☐ prone	☐ zeal
☐ devoted	☐ accumulate	☐ evaluation
☐ certification	☐ manage	☐ dogged
☐ ambitious	☐ bankruptcy	☐ formidable
☐ employ	☐ flawless	☐ workaholic
☐ incline	☐ strategy	
☐ consensus	☐ luminary	
☐ motto	☐ arena	
☐ profession	☐ compensate	
☐ fierce	☐ crew	

表中共有 127 个单词

您不确认的单词 _____ 个，占总数的 _____%

如果比例高于 10%，请耐心再复习一遍。如果比例低于 10%，您可以开始下一章的托福写作之旅了！

第三章

生活方式

reside [rɪˈzaɪd]

释义· *vi.* 居住；属于

例句· 在城里工作的人们实际上居住在临近的镇上。

People who work in the city actually reside in neighboring towns.

派生· resident *n.* 居民 *adj.* 居住的

residence *n.* 住宅；居住

搭配· 居住（大地点）；存在于；属于 reside in

居住（小地点）reside at

frugal [ˈfruːgl]

释义· *adj.* 节俭的；节约的；省钱的

例句· 我们小的时候就被教育要在生活中节俭和勤劳。

As children, we were taught to be frugal and hard-working in life.

同义· thrifty *adj.* 节约的

派生· frugality *n.* 节俭

搭配· 俭朴的个人生活 frugal private life

entertainment [ˌentər'teɪnmənt]

释义· *n.* 娱乐；款待

例句· 电视已经取代了电影，成为我国最大众化的娱乐形式。

Television has displaced film as our country's most popular form of entertainment.

同义· recreation *n.* 娱乐；消遣

搭配· 娱乐业 entertainment industry

accommodation [əˌkɑːmə'deɪʃn]

释义· *n.* 住处；调和；和解

例句· 食物、衣服和住所是生活的必需品。

Food, clothes and accommodation are all necessary for living.

同根· accommodating *adj.* 随和的；乐于助人的

edification [ˌedɪfɪ'keɪʃn]

释义· *n.* (U) 教诲；启迪；熏陶

例句· 生活中，我们要听从父母的教诲，不断地积累经验。

We need to follow our parents' edification and accumulate experience constantly in life.

cradle ['kreɪdl]

释义· *n.* 发源地；摇篮 *vt.* 轻轻抱着

例句· 一位著名的艺术家曾说过，生活是一切灵感的来源。

A famous artist once said that life is the cradle of all inspirations.

搭配· 某物的发源地 cradle of sth.

在摇篮里；在婴儿时期；初期　in the cradle

从生到死；一辈子　from the cradle to the grave

economical [ˌiːkəˈnɑːmɪkl]

释义· *adj.* 经济的；节约的；省钱的

例句· 在网上购物对于大部分居民来说是一种经济划算的消费方式。

Shopping online is an economical pattern of consumption for most citizens.

搭配· 经济实惠　economical and practical

venue [ˈvenjuː]

释义· *n.* 聚会地点（如音乐厅、体育比赛场馆、会场）

例句· 那支乐队将在尽可能多的地方演出。

The band will play as many venues as possible.

decorative [ˈdekəreɪtɪv]

释义· *adj.* 装饰性的；作装饰用的

例句· 这间房子里有很多装饰性的植物和绘画。

This room is filled with many decorative plants and paintings.

同根· decorate *v.* 装饰；布置

decoration *n.* 装饰；装饰品

fulfillment [fʊlˈfɪlmənt]

释义· *n.* (U) 满足（感）；履行；实行

例句· 只有基本的生活需求得到满足，人们才会追求精神上的享受。

Only after the essential fulfillment is met will people seek for spiritual enjoyment.

elaborate [ɪˈlæbərət]

释义· *adj.* 精心制作的；详尽的

例句· 这份精心制作的蛋糕是她收到的最好的生日礼物。

This elaborate cake is the best gift she has ever received.

搭配· 详细说明 elaborate on

extravagant [ɪkˈstrævəgənt]

释义· *adj.* 奢侈的；浪费的；过分的

例句· 奢侈的生活方式是大部分中产阶级家庭所无法承受的。

Most middle-class families cannot support the extravagant lifestyle.

同义· lavish *adj.* 铺张的；奢侈的

搭配· 奢望 extravagant hope

instructive [ɪnˈstrʌktɪv]

释义· *adj.* 有益的；有启发性的；教育性的

例句· 在自行车上看城市，总是给予我愉快而有益的体验。

Seeing cities from on top of a bike is both pleasurable and instructive.

同根· instruction *n.* 命令；指示

costly [ˈkɔːstli]

释义· *adj.* 昂贵的；代价大的

例句· 如果你想过上富裕的生活，就得承担得起昂贵的房价和其他费用。

If you want to live affluently, you must afford costly housing price and other expenses.

domestic [dəˈmestɪk]

释义· *adj.* 家用的；国内的；驯养的

例句· 父亲用这个月的工资买了很多新的家用电器。
The father spent his wage this month on some new domestic appliances.

派生· domesticate *v.* 驯养；教化；引进

搭配· 国内事务　domestic affairs
家庭暴力　domestic violence
国内生产总值　Gross Domestic Product (GDP)

exquisite [ɪk'skwɪzɪt]

释义· *adj.* 精致的；微妙的；剧烈的

例句· 这家饭店虽然不大，但食物和服务都很精致。
This restaurant is not spacious, but the food and service are exquisite.

派生· exquisiteness *n.* 优美；精湛

搭配· 小巧玲珑　small and exquisite

inspiration [ˌɪnspə'reɪʃn]

释义· *n.* 灵感；鼓舞

例句· 乡下生活的经历为这位画家提供了宝贵的灵感。
The experience of living in the countryside provides the valuable inspiration for this artist.

abstract ['æbstrækt]

释义· *adj.* 抽象的；纯理论的 *n.* 摘要；概要

例句· 他的描述过于抽象，以至于大家都不明白他说的是什么。
His description is too abstract that no one understands what he is talking about.

派生· abstracted *adj.* 心不在焉的

搭配· 抽象地；理论上　in the abstract

抽象派 abstract art

concrete ['kɑːŋkriːt]

释义· *adj.* 具体的；实在的；有形的 *v.* 凝结 *n.* (U) 混凝土

例句· 生活是抽象的艺术，数学是具体的艺术。

Life is the art of abstract, and Math is the art of concrete.

派生· concreteness *n.* 具体

搭配· 实际上；具体地 in the concrete

wealthy ['welθi]

释义· *adj.* 富有的；富裕的

例句· 他们基本上是一些非常有钱有势的精英。

They were, by and large, a very wealthy, privileged elite.

同义· rich *adj.* 富有的；肥沃的；昂贵的

affluent *adj.* 富裕的；流畅的

搭配· 有钱人 the wealthy

> **扩展** 三种"财富"的区别：
>
> treasure 作"财富"之意时，主要指的是"金银财宝"。
>
> wealth 既可以指物质上的财富，也可以指精神上的财富。
>
> possession 主要强调对财富的所有权。

preserve [prɪ'zɜːrv]

释义· *vt.* 腌制（食物）；保存 *n.* 保护区

例句· 我喜欢做果泥，只需要用一点糖把李子腌一下。

I like to make puree, using only enough sugar to preserve the plums.

派生· preserver *n.* 保护人；防腐剂

preservation *n.* 保存

precious ['preʃəs]

释义· *adj.* 宝贵的；珍贵的

例句· 这次的志愿者活动为他在进入职场前提供了宝贵的经验。

This volunteer activity offers him the precious experience before he enters the job market.

esteem [ɪ'stiːm]

释义· *vt.* 尊重；认为 *n.* (U) 尊重；尊敬

例句· 尊老爱幼是一项传统的生活美德。

To esteem the old and to cherish the young is a traditional virtue in life.

搭配· 为……而尊敬（某人）esteem for (sb.)

非常尊敬某人 hold sb. in high esteem

worthless ['wɜːrθləs]

释义· *adj.* 没用的；无价值的

例句· 这房子里堆满了没用的东西。

The house was full of worthless junk.

同根· worthful *adj.* 有价值的；可贵的

worthy *adj.* 值得的；配得上的

monitor ['mɑːnɪtər]

释义· *n.* 监视器；显示屏；班长 *v.* 监控；监视

例句· 现如今，生活中到处都是监视器，人们很难保持完全的隐私。

Nowadays, monitors are everywhere in life so that people hardly can keep total privacy.

custom ['kʌstəm]

释义· *n.* 风俗；习惯 *adj.* 订制的

例句· 钟努力去适应当地的风俗习惯。

Chung has tried to adapt to local customs.

派生· customize *vt.* 订做

customarily *adv.* 通常；习惯上

搭配· 做某事的习俗 the custom of doing sth.

misfortune [ˌmɪsˈfɔːrtʃuːn]

释义· *n.* (U) 不幸

例句· 我们不能被生活中的不幸打倒，相反，我们应该保持乐观。

We cannot be defeated by the misfortune in life; instead, we should be optimistic.

习语· 祸不单行。 Misfortunes never come alone.

vulnerable [ˈvʌlnərəbl]

释义· *adj.* 易患病的；易受伤害的；易受攻击的

例句· 老年人和婴儿易患各种疾病。

Old people and babies are vulnerable to all kinds of diseases.

派生· vulnerability *n.* 弱点；易损性

搭配· 易受……的伤害 be vulnerable to sth.

弱势群体 vulnerable group

relative [ˈrelətɪv]

释义· *n.* 亲戚；同类事物 *adj.* 相对的；比较的

例句· 这个人非常地自私和冷漠，他的亲戚朋友们都离开了他。

This man was very selfish and indifferent, and at last, his relatives and friends abandoned him.

搭配· 相对于；涉及 relative to

etiquette [ˈetɪket]

释义· *n.* (U) 礼仪；规矩

例句· 从小我们的父母就教育我们要遵守餐桌礼仪。

We were taught to obey the table etiquette by our parents from childhood.

搭配· 礼仪风俗 etiquette and custom

commuter [kəˈmjuːtər]

释义· *n.*（远距离）上下班往返的人

例句· 很多人都是开车上班族，但实际上骑自行车上班是一种更健康的方式。

Many people are car commuters, but actually, biking is a healthier way to go to the office.

搭配· 上下班时间 commuter time

交通中枢 commuter area

edible [ˈedəbl]

释义· *adj.* 可食用的

例句· 生活的常识告诉我们，这些蘑菇可以吃，但那些鲜艳的有毒。

The common sense in life tells us that these mushrooms are edible, but those bright-colored are poisonous.

反义· inedible *adj.* 不可食用的

property [ˈprɑːpərti]

释义· *n.* 财物；财产；性质

例句· 宾馆对住客个人财物的丢失或损坏概不负责。

The hotel is not responsible for any loss or damage to guests' personal property.

搭配· 产权 property right

不动产 real property

地产开发商 property developer

impoverished [ɪmˈpɑːvərɪʃt]

释义· *adj.* 贫穷的；枯竭的

例句· 这个穷困的大学生为了支付学费，每天都做兼职。

This impoverished university student took a part-time job every day to afford his tuition.

同根· impoverishment *n.* 贫穷

liberal [ˈlɪbərəl]

释义· *adj.* 开明的；自由的；慷慨的

例句· 我的父母很开明，允许我按照自己的方式生活。

My parents are quite liberal, allowing me to live in my way.

派生· liberalize *vt.* 使自由化

liberality *n.* 慷慨

liberalism *n.* 自由主义

jealousy [ˈdʒeləsi]

释义· *n.* 嫉妒；羡慕

例句· 他很快发现，在乡村生活中，人们狭隘善妒，喜欢传播流言蜚语。

He quickly discovered the petty jealousies and gossip of village life.

同义· envy *n.* 嫉妒

搭配· 一阵嫉妒 a pang/stab/twinge of jealousy

tempting [ˈtemptɪŋ]

释义· *adj.* 诱人的；吸引人的

例句· 电子游戏对青少年很有诱惑力，以至于有些人沉迷其中。

Video games are so tempting to the teenager that some people are addicted to them.

同根· temptation *n.* 引诱；诱惑物

generosity [ˌdʒenəˈrɑːsəti]

释义 · *n.* (U) 慷慨；大方；宽宏大量

例句 · 他经常向慈善机构捐献巨款，这体现了他的慷慨大方。

He often gave the massive amounts of money to charities, which shows his generosity.

pursuit [pərˈsuːt]

释义 · *n.* 追求；追赶；事业；消遣

例句 · 对自由和幸福的追求是所有人生活的最终目标。

The pursuit of liberty and happiness is the final goal of everyone's life.

visual [ˈvɪʒuəl]

释义 · *adj.* 视觉的

例句 · 很多人看电影是为了享受逼真的视觉效果。

Many people watch movies to enjoy realistic visual effects.

派生 · visually *adv.* 看得见地；形象化地；外表上

charity [ˈtʃærəti]

释义 · *n.* 慈善；慈善机构；宽容

例句 · 这次音乐会筹得的钱款将全部用于慈善事业。

All the money raised by the concert will go to charity.

搭配 · 义卖 charity sale

义演 charity performance

慈善事业 charity cause

rural [ˈrʊrəl]

释义 · *adj.* 乡村的；农村的

例句 · 他向往乡村生活，所以他辞掉了工作，搬到了乡下去住。

He yearned for rural life, so he quitted his job and moved to the countryside.

派生 · rurality *n.* 田园风光；田园生活

urban ['ɜːrbən]

释义 · *adj.* 城市的；都市的

例句 · 这座城市的大部分城区都紧邻公园，空气非常清新。

In this city, most urban areas are close to the park, so the air is fresh.

派生 · urbanization *n.* 城市化

urbanize *vt.* 使都市化

urbane *adj.* 彬彬有礼的

搭配 · 城市扩张　urban sprawl

amble ['æmbl]

释义 · *vi.* 漫步

例句 · 晚上，市民们在河边散步。

Citizens came out and ambled along the river in the evening.

miserable ['mɪzrəbl]

释义 · *adj.* 非常难受的；痛苦的；可怜的

例句 · 汤姆那个周末的心情非常糟糕，因为他父母不让他出去玩。

Tom spent the weekend feeling miserable for his parents didn't allow him to play outside.

philanthropy [fɪ'lænθrəpi]

释义 · *n.* (U) 慈善；博爱

例句 · 这名商人自从退休之后就热衷于慈善，并成立了自己的组织。

This businessman devoted himself to philanthropy after retirement and established his organization.

派生· philanthropic *adj.* 博爱的；仁慈的
　　　philanthropist *n.* 慈善家；乐善好施者

meditate ['medɪteɪt]

释义· *vt.* 考虑；计划；企图 *vi.* 冥想；沉思
例句· 他考虑了很久，决定和家人一起在澳大利亚度假。
　　　He meditated for a long time, deciding to spend the holiday with his family in Australia.
派生· mediation *n.* 冥想；沉思
　　　meditative *adj.* 冥想的；沉思的
搭配· 沉思某事　meditate on/upon sth.

irresistible [ˌɪrɪˈzɪstəbl]

释义· *adj.* 不可抗拒的；不可抵抗的；极为诱人的
例句· 美食是一种不可抗拒的诱惑，但保持均衡的饮食更重要。
　　　Gourmet is an irresistible temptation, but keeping a balanced diet is more important.
搭配· 不可抗力　irresistible force

excursion [ɪkˈskɜːrʒn]

释义· *n.* 短途旅行；远足；（短期的）涉足
例句· 这次旅游包括大峡谷观光。
　　　Included in the tour is an excursion to the Great Canyon.
搭配· 涉足 / 涉猎某事　excursion into sth.
　　　去远足；去短途旅行　on an excursion

ingredient [ɪnˈgriːdiənt]

释义· *n.* 组成部分；要素；原料
例句· 困难和挑战是生活中不可缺少的组成部分。
　　　Difficulties and challenges are the indispensable ingredients

of life.

encounter [ɪnˈkaʊntər]

释义· v. 遇到；遭遇；偶然碰见 n. 相遇；邂逅

例句· 尽管她遇到了很多困难，她也始终没有放弃对生活的希望。
Although she encountered many difficulties, she never gave up hope for life.

搭配· 遇到某人 / 遭遇某事 encounter with sb./sth.

exotic [ɪgˈzɑːtɪk]

释义· adj. 奇异的；异国的；外来的

例句· 她走遍了全世界所有具有奇异风情的地方。
She travels to all kinds of exotic locations all over the world.

relic [ˈrelɪk]

释义· n. 遗迹；纪念物

例句· 很多游客来到北京就是为了欣赏中国古代的遗迹。
Plenty of tourists visit Beijing only to appreciate the relics of ancient China.

搭配· 文物保护 relics protection
文物；文化遗产 cultural relic

recreation [ˌrekriˈeɪʃn]

释义· n. 娱乐；消遣

例句· 他全部的娱乐方式就是喝啤酒和看足球比赛。
His only recreations are drinking beer and watching football.

派生· recreational adj. 娱乐的；消遣的

monotonous [məˈnɑːtənəs]

释义· adj. 单调乏味的；毫无变化的

例句· 生活本身并不单调，如果你认为生活索然无味，那是因为你只是安于现状。

Life itself is not monotonous. If you think life is dull, you may just be satisfied with the status quo.

同根· monotony *n.* 单调；千篇一律

exterior [ɪk'stɪriər]

释义· *n.* 外部 *adj.* 外部的；外表的

例句· 这座建筑物在外观上是一项建筑杰作，精美雅致。

The exterior of the building was a masterpiece of architecture, elegant and graceful.

athletic [æθ'letɪk]

释义· *adj.* 健壮的；运动的

例句· 他每天都健身，所以虽然他已经 40 岁了，却有着 20 岁一般的健壮身体。

He exercises every day, so even though he is 40, he has a 20-year-old's athletic body.

搭配· 运动场；田径场地　athletic field

portable ['pɔːrtəbl]

释义· *adj.* 便携式的；手提的；轻便的

例句· 我们家购置了很多便携式设备。

Our home purchased some portable equipment.

派生· portability *n.* 可携带性；轻便

trend [trend]

释义· *n.* 趋势；倾向 *v.* 趋向

例句· 一个令人担心的趋势是，暴力行为的受害者越来越年轻，所以我们要在生活中注意自我保护。

A disturbing trend is that victims of violence are getting younger. Therefore, we should notice the self-protection of life.

搭配· 有……的趋势 trend to

向某方面发展的趋势 trend towards sth.

开创潮流 set the trend

流行的 on trend

prejudice ['predʒudɪs]

释义· *n.* 偏见；成见 *vt.* 使有偏见；损害

例句· 在游历了这个国家之后，他消除了对它的偏见。

After a journey of this country, he eliminated the prejudice against it.

派生· prejudicial *adj.* 不利的；有害的；引起偏见的

搭配· 对某人 / 某物的偏见 prejudice against sb./sth.

对某人 / 某物的好感 prejudice in favor of sb./sth.

tranquil ['træŋkwɪl]

释义· *adj.* 安静的；平静的；安宁的

例句· 他们在这个宁静的小村庄里度过了一个完美的假期。

They spent a perfect holiday in this small tranquil village.

派生· tranquility *n.* 宁静

tranquilize *vt.* 使安静；使平静

endure [ɪn'dʊr]

释义· *vt.* 忍受；忍耐 *vi.* 持续；持久

例句· 他再也无法忍受生活中的压力，最终开枪自杀了。

He could not endure the pressure from life anymore and shot himself in the end.

派生· endurance *n.* 忍耐力；忍耐

endurable *adj.* 能忍耐的；能持久的

搭配· 忍受做某事 endure doing sth.

consumer [kən'suːmər]

释义· *n.* 消费者；用户；顾客

例句· 消费者的需求促使制成品的进口量增加了。

Consumer demand led to higher imports of manufactured goods.

同根· consumption *n.* 消费

consuming *adj.* 令人着迷的；强烈的

identity [aɪ'dentəti]

释义· *n.* 身份；一致；特性

例句· 在生活中和工作中，每个人都需要明确自己的身份、职责和义务。

In life and work, everyone should confirm his or her identity, responsibility and duty.

同根· identical *adj.* 完全相同的

搭配· 身份证 identity card

amateur ['æmətər]

释义· *n.* 业余爱好者 *adj.* 业余爱好的

例句· 杰克是一位业余绘画爱好者，他画画只是因为喜欢。

Jack is an amateur who paints because he feels like it.

派生· amateurish *adj.* 业余的；外行的

relief [rɪ'liːf]

释义· *n.* （不快过后的）宽慰，轻松；解脱；消除

例句· 经过这次观光游，我如释重负，大感欣慰。

After this tour, I felt a massive surge of relief and happiness.

派生· relieve *vt.* 解除；减轻
搭配· 某物的消除　relieve of sth.
　　　救济金　relief fund

esthetic [es'θetɪk]

释义· *adj.* 美的；审美的 *n.* 美感；审美观
例句· 消费者都喜欢这类产品，因为它们外形美观且经久耐用、质量上乘。
　　　Consumers like these products for their esthetic appeal as well as their durability and quality.
同根· esthetics *n.* 美学

overweight [,oʊvər'weɪt]

释义· *adj.* 超重的；太胖的
例句· 即使是轻度超重也会增加患高血压的风险。
　　　Being even moderately overweight increases your risk of developing high blood pressure.

obesity [oʊ'biːsəti]

释义· *n.* (U) 肥胖；肥大
例句· 超重和肥胖会增加患心脏病和癌症的风险。
　　　Overweight and obesity increase the risk of heart disease and cancer.

dilemma [dɪ'lemə]

释义· *n.* （进退两难的）窘境，困境
例句· 许多女性面临着是出去工作还是照顾家庭的两难境地。
　　　Many women are faced with the dilemma of choosing between work and family.
搭配· 处于进退两难的境地　to be in a dilemma

greasy ['gri:si]

释义· *adj.* 油腻的；多脂的；圆滑的

例句· 太油腻的食物对我们的健康有害。

Too much greasy food is harmful to our health.

exhaust [ɪɡ'zɔ:st]

释义· *v.* 使筋疲力尽；耗尽；详尽讨论 *n.* 废气；排气管

例句· 他把所有的箱子搬到了楼上，把自己弄得筋疲力尽。

He'd exhausted himself carrying all the boxes upstairs.

派生· exhausted *adj.* 疲惫的；耗尽的

exhaustive *adj.* 详尽的；彻底的

exhaustible *adj.* 可被用尽的；会枯竭的

搭配· 废气　exhaust gas

recollection [ˌrekə'lekʃn]

释义· *n.* 记忆；回忆；回忆的事

例句· 我清楚地记得这部电影，其中一些电影片段在我的脑海里闪现。

I have a vivid recollection of this movie, some movie clips replaying in my mind.

搭配· 不记得（做过）某事　have no recollection of (doing) sth.

牢记在某人记忆中　embedded in one's recollection

如果我没记错的话　to the best of my recollection

initiative [ɪ'nɪʃətɪv]

释义· *n.* 主动性；积极性；主动权

例句· 我们不能依靠别人来解决生活中的问题，有时要发挥自己的主动性。

We cannot rely on others to solve problems in life; sometimes we should take our initiative.

搭配 · 采取行动；带头 take the initiative

某人自己主动地 on one's own initiative

invigorated [ɪnˈvɪɡəreɪtɪd]

释义 · *adj.* 精力充沛的；生机勃勃的

例句 · 只要你对生活充满希望，你每天都会充满活力。

As long as you have hope for life, you will be invigorated every day.

readily [ˈredɪli]

释义 · *adv.* 容易地；乐意地；便利地

例句 · 这些信息在网上一查就能找到。

The information is readily accessible on the Internet.

decay [dɪˈkeɪ]

释义 · *v.* （建筑、地方等）破败；腐烂 *n.* (U) 衰退；腐烂

例句 · 数百座古建筑任由破败，却形成了一种独特的美。

Hundreds of historic buildings are being allowed to decay, and form unique beauty.

搭配 · 破败；腐朽 fall into decay

nutritious [nuˈtrɪʃəs]

释义 · *adj.* 有营养的；营养丰富的

例句 · 这本食谱里有许多简单但营养价值很高的膳食。

The cookbook contains many simple but highly nutritious meals.

同根 · nutritional *adj.* 营养的

leisure [ˈliːʒər]

释义 · *n.* (U) 空闲；闲暇；休闲

例句· 旅行是消磨空闲时间的一种放松方式。
Traveling is a relaxing way to kill the leisure time.

搭配· 悠闲；不慌不忙　at leisure
休闲活动　leisure activity

spoil [spɔɪl]

释义· v. 宠坏；溺爱；破坏 n. 战利品

例句· 她的父母简直把她宠坏了，就因为她是独生女。
Her parents spoiled her badly only because she is the only child.

同义· dote v. 溺爱
pamper v. 纵容

扩展· spoilt/spoiled (过去式) spoilt/spoiled (过去分词)

ameliorate [ə'mi:liəreɪt]

释义· v. 改善；改进

例句· 如何改善空气质量是现在市民们最关注的问题之一。
How to ameliorate the air condition is one of the most important issues that most citizens are concerned about now.

confuse [kən'fju:z]

释义· vt. (将……) 混淆；使迷惑

例句· 我认为把书本同生活混为一谈是大错特错。
I think it's a serious mistake to confuse books with life.

派生· confusion n. 混淆；困惑
confused adj. 困惑的；混乱的；糊涂的

搭配· 将 A 和 B 混淆　confuse A and/with B

sustainable [sə'steɪnəbl]

释义· adj. 可持续的；不破坏生态平衡的

例句· 人们不能光顾眼前的生活，还要想着可持续发展，着眼于未来。

People cannot only focus on the presence of life but also to be sustainable, they have to think of the future.

派生· sustainability *n.* 持续性

搭配· 可持续发展 sustainable development

routine [ru:'ti:n]

释义· *n.* 日常工作；例行公事 *adj.* 日常的；例行的；平淡的

例句· 穿衣打扮是我们每天都要干的事情。

Dressing is a task which we do every day as a matter of routine.

搭配· 日常生活；日常工作 daily routine

addict ['ædɪkt]

释义· *n.* 对……入迷的人；吸毒成瘾者

例句· 我侄女绝对是个电子游戏迷，每天至少要玩 5 个小时的游戏。

My niece is a complete video game addict, spending at least 5 hours on games each day.

派生· addicted *adj.* 入迷的；上瘾的

addictive *adj.* 使人上瘾的

搭配· 吸毒者；滥用药物者 drug addict

necessity [nə'sesəti]

释义· *n.* 必需品；需要

例句· 洗衣机和书都是生活必需品，前者是物质上的，后者是精神上的。

The washing machine and the book are necessities for life, and the former is for physical, latter for mental.

搭配· 必然地 of necessity

不得已；必然地 by necessity

出于需要　out of necessity

fragile ['frædʒl]

释义· *adj.* 脆弱的；易碎的

例句· 老年人因骨骼比较脆弱，更容易受重伤。

Old people are more likely to be seriously injured because their bones are fragile.

partial ['pɑːrʃl]

释义· *adj.* 部分的；偏爱的；偏袒的

例句· 这座城市内部分地区禁止使用私家车。

There is a partial ban on the use of private cars in this city.

派生· partiality *n.* 偏心；偏爱；癖好

搭配· 偏爱某物　be partial to sth.

balance ['bæləns]

释义· *n.* 平衡；余额 *v.* 使保持平衡；结算；抵消

例句· 要想生活得开心，就要尽量保持工作和娱乐的平衡。

If you want a happy life, you should try to keep a balance between work and play.

派生· balanced *adj.* 平衡的；和谐的

搭配· 总的来说　on balance

（结果）悬而未决；（前途）不明朗　be/hang in the balance

amuse [ə'mjuːz]

释义· *vt.* 消遣；娱乐

例句· 当你觉得有压力时，你需要分散注意力、消遣一下，这样就不会总想着工作的事了。

When feeling stressed, you need distractions and amuse yourself, so you won't keep thinking about work.

派生· amusement *n.* 可笑；娱乐

amusing *adj.* 逗人笑的；有乐趣的

搭配· 自娱自乐 amuse oneself

游乐园 amusement park

priority [praɪˈɔːrəti]

释义· *n.* 优先事项；优先；优先权

例句· 考虑到能用的钱这么少，出国旅行的事情只好暂时放下了。

Given so little money available, traveling abroad must remain a low priority.

搭配· 优先考虑；给……优先权 give priority to

比……重要 take priority over

头等大事 first/top/main priority

分清事情的轻重缓急 get your priorities straight

costume [ˈkɑːstuːm]

释义· *n.* （某地或某历史时期的）服装；戏服

例句· 每个民族都有自己的民族服饰，它象征着当地的文化。

Every nation has a national costume which symbolizes the local culture.

搭配· 化妆舞会 costume ball

isolated [ˈaɪsəleɪtɪd]

释义· *adj.* 偏远的；孤零零的；孤独的；单独的

例句· 这个偏僻的地方有美丽的景色，但参观的人并不多。

This isolated spot has beautiful scenery, but not many people visit there.

同根· isolation *n.* 孤独；隔离；绝缘

fluctuation [ˌflʌktʃuˈeɪʃn]

释义· *n.* 波动；上下浮动

例句· 物价的波动会导致社会的不稳定。

The fluctuation of price would lead to social instability.

superficial [ˌsuːpərˈfɪʃl]

释义· *adj.* 肤浅的；表面的

例句· 大多数外国人对中国文化的了解是很浅显的，因为他们并没有来过中国。

Most foreigners only have the most superficial understanding of Chinese culture because they have never visited China in person.

派生· superficiality *n.* 肤浅；表面性的事物

搭配· 从表面上看 at/on a superficial level

preferable [ˈprefrəbl]

释义· *adj.* 更好的；更可取的；更合适的

例句· 在家庭聚会上，人们通常认为穿私服比穿正装更好。

At family parties, people usually think it is preferable to wear own clothes than to wear a suit.

搭配· 做某事更好的 be preferable to doing sth.

satisfaction [ˌsætɪsˈfækʃn]

释义· *n.* 满足；满意；赔偿

例句· 在生活中帮助别人解决问题能够得到极大的满足。

There is real satisfaction in helping other people to solve their problems in life.

同根· satisfactory *adj.* 满意的；符合要求的

搭配· 使某人满意 to sb.'s satisfaction

满意地 with satisfaction

innate [ɪˈneɪt]

释义· *adj.* 天生的；先天的；固有的

例句· 儿童的语言学习能力是天生的。

Children have an innate ability to learn the language.

派生· innateness *n.* 天赋；天生

搭配· 天生的能力；天赋才能 innate ability/capacity

available [əˈveɪləbl]

释义· *adj.* 可获得的；有空的；可用的

例句· 通过网络，我们可以在几天之内购得来自世界各地的商品。

Via the Internet, commodities from all over the world are available for us in a few days.

派生· availability *n.* 可用性；有效性

搭配· 可以用来……；对……有效 be available to/for

promising [ˈprɑːmɪsɪŋ]

释义· *adj.* 有希望的；有前途的

例句· 为了有一个光明的未来，他决定移民美国。

For a promising future, he decided to migrate to America.

cherish [ˈtʃerɪʃ]

释义· *vt.* 重视；珍视；怀有（感情等）

例句· 生活中我们必须注重每一个人的隐私，以避免不必要的麻烦。

We must cherish everyone's privacy in life to avoid unnecessary trouble.

派生· cherished *adj.* 珍爱的；珍藏的

expenditure [ɪk'spendɪtʃər]

释义· *n.* 支出；花费；费用

例句· 他非常喜欢收藏古董，在这上面的支出几乎花光了他的工资。

He likes collecting antique very much, and the expenditure of this almost consumes his wages.

convenience [kən'viːniəns]

释义· *n.* (U) 方便；便利的事物

例句· 为方便顾客，这家超市提供袋装服务。

The supermarket offers a bag-packing service, as a convenience to customers.

搭配· 为了……的方便 for the convenience of

便利商店 convenience store

handicap ['hændikæp]

释义· *vt.* 妨碍；阻碍 *n.* 生理缺陷；障碍；不利条件

例句· 他不会说英语，这使他无法享受他的英国之行。

He could not speak English, which handicapped him to enjoy his trip to Britain.

派生· handicapped *adj.* 残疾的；有生理缺陷的

搭配· 智力 / 生理 / 视力缺陷 mental/ physical/visual handicap

fatigue [fə'tiːg]

释义· *n.* (U) 疲劳；厌倦

例句· 生活的琐事使她身心俱疲。

Trifles in life made her suffer from physical and mental fatigue.

permanent ['pɜːrmənənt]

释义· *adj.* 永久的；永恒的 *n.* 卷发；烫发

例句· 酗酒能造成永久性大脑损伤。

Heavy drinking can cause permanent damage to the brain.

同根· permanence *n.* 持久；永久

搭配· 固定职业 permanent job

random ['rændəm]

释义· *adj.* 随机的；任意的；胡乱的 *n.* 随意；随机

例句· 生活中每天都会有很多随机的麻烦事，我们要学会灵活应对。

In daily life, there are many random troubles every day, so we need to know how to deal with them flexibly.

派生· randomness *n.* 随意；无安排

randomize *vt.* 使随机化

搭配· 随意；随机 at random

stereotype ['steriətaɪp]

释义· *n.* 模式化的形象（或特征）；固定模式 *vt.* 使模式化

例句· 人们对成功商人一直都有一种固定印象。

There has always been a stereotype of successful businessmen.

派生· stereotypical *adj.* 典型的；带有成见的

estimate ['estɪmət]

释义· *n.* 估计；估价 *v.* 估计；估价

例句· 我可以粗略估计一下你所需要的木材量。

I can give you a rough estimate of the amount of wood you will need.

派生· estimated *adj.* 估计的；预计的

搭配· 估计……；估计有…… estimate at

conventional [kən'venʃənl]

释义· *adj.* 传统的；惯例的
例句· 生活中总有些人坚持传统道德，有些人喜欢标新立异。
There always are some people believing in conventional morals and some doing something unorthodox.
同义· orthodox *adj.* 传统的；正统的
派生· conventionalism *n.* 墨守成规；传统主义
搭配· 大多数人的看法；普遍信念 conventional wisdom

prospect ['prɑːspekt]

释义· *n.* 希望；前景；景色 *v.* 勘探
例句· 他失业了，离婚了，生活对他来说没有希望了。
He lost his job and divorced so that life had no prospect for him.
派生· prospective *adj.* 未来的；预期的
搭配· 有做某事的希望 prospect of doing sth.
可以预料到；有希望 in prospect
前瞻研究 prospective study

aggressive [ə'gresɪv]

释义· *adj.* 有进取心的；好斗的；侵略性的
例句· 他是一位锐意进取、竞争意识很强的主管，颇受尊敬。
He is respected as a very aggressive and competitive executive.

outdated [ˌaʊt'deɪtɪd]

释义· *adj.* 过时的；陈旧的
例句· 因特网的出现使很多东西都过时了，比如 MP3。
The Internet made many things outdated, such as the MP3.

同义· old-fashioned 陈旧的；过时的

demoded *adj.* 过时的

senior ['si:niər]

释义· *adj.* 年长的；高级的；地位高的 *n.* 年长者；毕业班学生；上司

例句· 生活中我们要尊重老年人。

We must respect senior citizens in life.

搭配· 比……级别高；比……年长 be senior to

老年人 senior citizen

nostalgic [nə'stældʒɪk]

释义· *adj.* 怀旧的；恋旧的

例句· 看到那些学生时代的旧照片，我不禁产生了怀旧之情。

Seeing those old school photographs has made me feel quite nostalgic.

搭配· 怀旧的回忆；怀旧记忆 nostalgic memory

sophisticated [sə'fɪstɪkeɪtɪd]

释义· *adj.* 复杂的；精致的；久经世故的

例句· 生活本身并不复杂，是人们把简单的生活变得复杂了。

Life itself is not sophisticated at all, and it is people that make simple life complicated.

puzzle ['pʌzl]

释义· *v.* 对……苦苦思索；使困惑 *n.* 谜；难题

例句· 我一直在琢磨明天的旅行路线，但找个导游也许是更好的办法。

I have been puzzling over tomorrow's travel route, but to find a tour guide may be a better way.

派生· puzzled *adj.* 困惑的；迷惑不解的

搭配· 苦苦思索；仔细琢磨 puzzle over

琢磨出……的答案 puzzle out

amenity [ə'menəti]

释义· *n.* 便利设施；生活福利设施

例句· 该酒店位于市中心，紧邻商店和当地的便利设施。

The hotel is in the city center, close to shops and local amenities.

bustle ['bʌsl]

释义· *n.* (U) 忙乱嘈杂；喧闹 *v.* 四下忙碌；催促

例句· 梭罗在《没有原则的生活》一书中说道："这是个充满交易的世界，永远忙忙碌碌！"

In his essay *Life without Principle*, Thoreau wrote: "This world is a place of business. What an infinite bustle!"

搭配· 忙碌；东奔西跑 bustle about

赶快 bustle up

熙熙攘攘；忙碌 hustle and bustle

gossip ['gɑ:sɪp]

释义· *n.* (U) 流言蜚语；闲言碎语 *vi.* 传播流言蜚语；说三道四

例句· 关于他缺席的原因有很多传言。

There has been much gossip about the possible reasons for his absence.

派生· gossipy *adj.* 记述逸事的；喜欢说长道短的

搭配· 说……闲话 gossip about

prevalent ['prevələnt]

释义· *adj.* 普遍的；流行的

例句· 抽烟在年轻女性中变得越来越常见。

Smoking is becoming increasingly prevalent among younger

women.

派生· prevalence *n.* 流行；普遍

搭配· 流行趋势 prevalent trend

plausible ['plɔːzəbl]

释义· *adj.* （解释或说法）似乎真实的，貌似合理的

例句· 长辈们教给我们的一些常识听起来很有道理，但根本不实用。

Some common sense elders taught us just sounds plausible but not practical at all.

shelter ['ʃeltər]

释义· *n.* 避难所；庇护处；居所；遮蔽 *v.* 保护；躲避

例句· 无论我们在生活或工作中遇到什么困难，家永远是我们的避难所。

No matter what difficulties we meet in life or work, home is always our shelter.

派生· sheltered *adj.* 受到保护的；有遮蔽物的

搭配· 躲避某物 shelter from sth.

寻求庇护；避难 take shelter

obsolete [ˌɑːbsə'liːt]

释义· *adj.* 过时的；废弃的；淘汰的

例句· 许多年轻人每年都会购买最新款的智能手机，而一些家长仍在使用过时的手机。

Many young adults are buying the latest smart phones each year, while some parents are still using obsolete ones.

prevail [prɪ'veɪl]

释义· *vi.* 战胜；盛行；流行

例句· 内心的力量将促使你战胜生活中的困难。

Your inner strength will enable you to prevail over life's

obstacles.

派生· prevailing *adj.* 普遍的；流行的

搭配· 说服某人做某事 prevail on/upon sb. to do sth.

战胜某人 prevail against/over sb.

rational [ˈræʃnəl]

释义· *adj.* 理性的；合理的

例句· 当遇到问题时不要慌，要保持理性，这样才能尽可能避免错误。
When facing troubles, you need to be rational but not panic; thus you can avoid errors as far as possible.

反义· irrational *adj.* 不合逻辑的；没有道理的

派生· rationality *n.* 合理性

rationalize *v.* 使合理化

remote [rɪˈmoʊt]

释义· *adj.* 偏僻的；遥远的；疏远的 *n.* 远程

例句· 去年，他们去了一个偏远的边境小镇旅行，受到了当地人的款待。
Last year they traveled to a remote border town, and local people treated them.

派生· remoteness *n.* 偏远

搭配· 遥控；遥控器 remote control

释义	短语
中年危机	midlife crisis
过度保护的	ultra-protective
有氧运动	aerobic exercise
老龄化社会	aging/graying society
平均寿命	average life span
回顾	in retrospect
交通堵塞	traffic jam/congestion
视觉享受	visual enjoyment
从日常的琐事中摆脱出来	get away from the daily grind
根深蒂固的	deep-seated/inveterate
酒驾	drunk driving
摩天大楼	skyscraper
成就颇高的	high-achieving
跨文化交流	cross-cultural communication
主流文化	mainstream culture
慢性病	long-lasting diseases
萝卜青菜各有所爱	different strokes for different folks
久坐不动的生活方式	sedentary lifestyle

特效	special effects
让人放松	calm the nerve and restore the soul
艺术品味	artistic taste
饮食均衡	balanced diet
维生素和矿物质	vitamins and minerals
拆除	tear down
戴口罩	wear masks
空气过滤器	air filters
弘扬……	carry forward
（上下班的）交通高峰时间，交通拥挤时段	rush hour

巩 固 练 习

练习1 根据下面的中文释义，写出对应的单词（词组）。

A

有营养的 n_____

支出 e_____

方便 c_____

偏僻的 r_____

居住 r_____

偏远的 i_____

估计 e_____

希望 p_____

避难所 s_____

流行趋势 p_____

食品卫生 f_____

B

美的 e_____

窘境 d_____

旅游胜地 t_____

永久的 p_____

记忆 r_____

精力充沛的 i_____

交通堵塞 t_____

娱乐 e_____

抽象的 a_____

家用的 d_____

消费者 c_____

练习2 用方框中所给单词（词组）的适当形式填空。

tempting	accommodation	pursuit	prejudice against
relative	encounter	elaborate	exhaust
spoil	prevail over	inspiration	innate ability
puzzle over	endure	amuse	

1. Food, clothes and a_____（住所）are all necessary for living.

2. This e_____（精心制作的）cake is the best gift she has ever received.

3. The experience of living in the countryside provides the valuable i_____ (灵感) for this artist.

4. This man was very selfish and indifferent, and at last, his r_____ (亲戚) and friends abandoned him.

5. Video games are so t_____ (诱人的) to the teenager that some people are addicted to them.

6. The p_____ (追求) of liberty and happiness is the final goal of everyone's life.

7. Although she e_____ (遇到) many difficulties, she never gave up hope for life.

8. After a journey of this country, he eliminated the p_____ (偏见) it.

9. He could not e_____ (忍受) the pressure from life anymore and shot himself in the end.

10. He'd e_____ (使筋疲力尽) himself carrying all the boxes upstairs.

11. Her parents s_____ (宠坏) her badly only because she is the only child.

12. When feeling stressed, you need distractions and a_____ (消遣) yourself, so you won't keep thinking about work.

13. Children have an i_____ (天生的能力) to learn the language.

14. I have been p_____ (琢磨) tomorrow's travel route, but to find a tour guide may be a better way.

15. Your inner strength will enable you to p_____ (战胜) life's obstacles.

☐ reside	☐ monitor	☐ excursion
☐ frugal	☐ custom	☐ ingredient
☐ entertainment	☐ misfortune	☐ encounter
☐ accommodation	☐ vulnerable	☐ exotic
☐ edification	☐ relative	☐ relic
☐ cradle	☐ etiquette	☐ recreation
☐ economical	☐ commuter	☐ monotonous
☐ venue	☐ edible	☐ exterior
☐ decorative	☐ property	☐ athletic
☐ fulfillment	☐ impoverished	☐ portable
☐ elaborate	☐ liberal	☐ trend
☐ extravagant	☐ jealousy	☐ prejudice
☐ instructive	☐ tempting	☐ tranquil
☐ costly	☐ generosity	☐ endure
☐ domestic	☐ pursuit	☐ consumer
☐ exquisite	☐ visual	☐ identity
☐ inspiration	☐ charity	☐ amateur
☐ abstract	☐ rural	☐ relief
☐ concrete	☐ urban	☐ esthetic
☐ wealthy	☐ amble	☐ overweight
☐ preserve	☐ miserable	☐ obesity
☐ precious	☐ philanthropy	☐ dilemma
☐ esteem	☐ meditate	☐ greasy
☐ worthless	☐ irresistible	☐ exhaust

☐ recollection	☐ isolated	☐ outdated
☐ initiative	☐ fluctuation	☐ senior
☐ invigorated	☐ superficial	☐ nostalgic
☐ readily	☐ preferable	☐ sophisticated
☐ decay	☐ satisfaction	☐ puzzle
☐ nutritious	☐ innate	☐ amenity
☐ leisure	☐ available	☐ bustle
☐ spoil	☐ promising	☐ gossip
☐ ameliorate	☐ cherish	☐ prevalent
☐ confuse	☐ expenditure	☐ plausible
☐ sustainable	☐ convenience	☐ shelter
☐ routine	☐ handicap	☐ obsolete
☐ addict	☐ fatigue	☐ prevail
☐ necessity	☐ permanent	☐ rational
☐ fragile	☐ random	☐ remote
☐ partial	☐ stereotype	
☐ balance	☐ estimate	
☐ amuse	☐ conventional	
☐ priority	☐ prospect	
☐ costume	☐ aggressive	

表中共有 127 个单词

您不确认的单词 _____ 个，占总数的 _____%

如果比例高于 10%，请耐心再复习一遍。如果比例低于 10%，您可以开始下一章的托福写作之旅了！

人群品质

sociable ['souʃəbl]

释义· *adj.* 好交际的；合群的；友善的

例句· 一些生物学家得出一个有些令人吃惊的结论：婴儿天生好交际，而且乐于助人。

The somewhat surprising answer at which some biologists have arrived is that babies are innately sociable and helpful to others.

反义· unsociable *adj.* 不爱交际的；不合群的

派生· sociability *n.* 善于交际；社交性

abnormal [æb'nɔːrml]

释义· *adj.* 不正常的；反常的；变态的

例句· 我父母认为一个男孩子对芭蕾舞感兴趣并不正常。

My parents thought it was abnormal for a boy to be interested in ballet.

派生· abnormality *n.* 反常；畸形；变态

搭配· 异常现象　abnormal phenomena

异常行为　abnormal behavior

loyalty [ˈlɔɪəlti]

释义· n. 忠诚；忠实

例句· 对我们中的大多数人来说，友谊是我们学习忠诚和谨慎的地方。

For many of us, friendships are the place where we learn about loyalty and discretion.

搭配· 品牌忠诚度　brand loyalty

absurd [əbˈsɜːrd]

释义· adj. 荒谬的；荒唐的

例句· 暗示说他们知道怎么回事但却袖手旁观是荒谬的。

It's absurd to suggest that they knew what was going on but did nothing.

cooperative [koʊˈɑːpərətɪv]

释义· adj. 合作的；协作的 n. 合作企业

例句· 在合作小组中，成员们更是常常能够独自产生新的想法、发现新策略和找到新的解决方案。

In cooperative groups, members more frequently generate new ideas, strategies, and solutions that they would think of on their own.

搭配· 合作学习　cooperative learning

合作伙伴　cooperative partner

affection [əˈfekʃn]

释义· n. (U) 钟爱；喜爱

例句· 她逐渐对这个地方钟爱有加。

She had developed quite an affection for the place.

betray [bɪ'treɪ]

释义· *vt.* 辜负；背叛；出卖

例句· 如果我告诉某人我不会辜负他的信任，我就会恪守诺言。
When I tell someone I will not betray his confidence I keep
my word.

派生· betrayal *n.* 背叛；辜负；出卖

搭配· 向 B 出卖 A betray A to B
原形毕露；无意中露出本性 betray oneself

organized ['ɔːrgənaɪzd]

释义· *adj.* 有条理的；有组织的；有安排的

例句· 这些人做事效率很高，井井有条，还是时间管理高手。
These people are very efficient, very organized, and excellent
time managers.

反义· unorganized *adj.* 无组织的；无系统的；杂乱无章的

搭配· 井然有序 be well organized

appreciate [ə'priːʃieɪt]

释义· *vt.* 感激；欣赏；理解 *vi.* 增值

例句· 当我最需要的时候，彼得在我身边支持我。我将永存感激。
Peter stood by me when I most needed it. I'll always
appreciate that.

派生· appreciative *adj.* 感激的；赏识的

搭配· 感激做某事 appreciate doing sth.

vain [veɪn]

释义· *adj.* 自负的；徒劳的；无结果的

例句· 她很漂亮，但她是如此地骄傲和自负，不能忍受任何人超越她的
美丽。

She was beautiful but so proud and vain that she could not
endure anyone who surpass her in beauty.

派生· vainglorious *adj.* 非常自负的；自命不凡的

搭配· 枉费心机；徒劳无益；白费力气 in vain

arbitrary ['ɑːrbətreri]

释义· *adj.* 武断的；专横的；任意的

例句· 鲁莽的人经常做出武断的决定。

A reckless man often makes an arbitrary decision.

mutual ['mjuːtʃuəl]

释义· *adj.* 相互的；共同的

例句· 互相尊重是任何一种伙伴关系成功建立的必要条件。

Mutual respect is necessary for any partnership to work.

派生· mutuality *n.* 相互关系

搭配· 相互协商 / 双方同意 mutual agreement/consent

共同的朋友 / 兴趣 mutual friend/interest

互惠互利 mutual benefit

相互的理解 mutual understanding

temperament ['temprəmənt]

释义· *n.* 性格；气质

例句· 他容易冲动，经常因此惹麻烦。

His impulsive temperament regularly got him into difficulties.

派生· temperamental *adj.* 喜怒无常的；气质的

搭配· 艺术气质 artistic temperament

astute [ə'stuːt]

释义· *adj.* 机敏的；精明的；狡猾的

例句· 此时此刻，我们最需要的是历史的远见、博大的胸襟、机敏的智慧和果敢的决断。

At this juncture, we need historical insight, cross-board vision, astute wisdom and resolute decision.

派生· astuteness *n.* 精明；机敏

搭配· 敏锐的判断力 astute judgment

awkward ['ɔ:kwərd]

释义· *adj.* 令人尴尬的；使人难堪的；棘手的

例句· 笑可以助人化解尴尬。

A laugh can help people escape an awkward situation.

派生· awkwardness *n.* 尴尬；笨拙

congenial [kən'dʒi:niəl]

释义· *adj.* 意气相投的；相宜的；适合的

例句· 我发现班里有几个同学和我挺投缘。

I found quite a few classmates congenial to me.

搭配· 宜人的环境 congenial atmosphere/surroundings/ environment

意气相投的伙伴 congenial company

sincere [sɪn'sɪr]

释义· *adj.* 真诚的；诚挚的

例句· 我想对曾经帮助和支持过我的人说一声衷心的感谢。

I would like to say a sincere "thank you" to everyone who has helped and supported me.

反义· insincere *adj.* 不诚恳的；不真心的

派生· sincerity *n.* 真实；诚挚

搭配· 诚心诚意 sincere desire

诚挚的谢意 sincere thanks/gratitude

扩展· sincerer（比较级）sincerest（最高级）

bewilder [bɪˈwɪldər]

释义· *vt.* 使迷惑；使不知所措

例句· 富贵不能淫，贫贱不能移，威武不能屈。

Wealth cannot bewilder one's mind; poverty cannot undermine one's moral integrity, and force cannot seize one's dignity.

派生· bewildering *adj.* 令人困惑的；使人糊涂的

bewilderment *n.* 困惑；迷惘

spouse [spaʊs]

释义· *n.* 配偶

例句· 如果我们自己都不了解自己，那么我们的配偶，或就此而言任何人，又怎么能够理解我们?

How can our spouse, or anyone for that matter, understand us if we don't know how we feel ourselves?

candid [ˈkændɪd]

释义· *adj.* 坦白的；直率的

例句· 双方互信是此种关系的基础，一旦信任被打破，坦白公正的对话是不可能的。

Mutual trust is the basis of such relations and once that trust is breached, candid conversations are less likely.

搭配· 敢说直话的朋友；诤友 candid friend

baffle [ˈbæfl]

释义· *vt.* 使困惑；难倒

例句· 朋友们夸我独立自主，这常使我很疑惑，但现在我明白他们的意思了。

Friends would compliment me on my independence, which used to baffle me, but now I can see what they meant.

派生· baffling *adj.* 令人困惑的

bafflement *n.* 困惑；不解

hesitant ['hezɪtənt]

释义· *adj.* 不愿的；犹豫的；迟疑不决的

例句· 她不大愿意站出来讲述自己的经历。

She was hesitant about coming forward with her story.

同根· hesitance *n.* 犹豫；踌躇

搭配· 对……犹豫不决 be hesitate about sth.

吞吞吐吐 hesitate in

contemptuous [kən'temptʃuəs]

释义· *adj.* 鄙视的；表示轻蔑的

例句· 他公开对自己的父亲表示鄙视。

He was openly contemptuous of his father.

搭配· 鄙视某人 / 某物 be contemptuous of sb./sth.

轻蔑的言词 contemptuous remarks

greed [gri:d]

释义· *n.* (U) 贪婪；贪心

例句· 贪婪可以灭绝人性和良知。

Greed suffocates humanity and conscience.

同义· avarice *n.* 贪婪

派生· greedy *adj.* 贪婪的；贪吃的；渴望的

elegant ['elɪgənt]

释义· *adj.* 高雅的；优美的；巧妙的；简洁的

例句· 帕特里夏看上去跟往常一样美丽优雅。

Patricia looked beautiful and elegant as always.

派生· elegance *n.* 典雅；高雅

搭配· 美观大方　elegant appearance

风采　elegant demeanor

casual ['kæʒuəl]

释义· *adj.* 随便的；非正式的；临时的

例句· 她对待生活的态度很随便。

She had a casual attitude to life.

搭配· 漫不经心的样子　a casual manner

临时工　casual labor/worker

便装　casual clothes

envy ['envi]

释义· *v.* 羡慕；忌妒 *n.* (U) 忌妒

例句· 我不羡慕那些已经成为电视超级明星、对其他却一无所知的年轻人。

I don't envy the young ones who've become TV superstars and know no other world.

派生· envious *adj.* 羡慕的；嫉妒的

搭配· 成为某人 / 某物羡慕的对象　be the envy of sb./sth.

一阵嫉妒　a twinge/pang of envy

出于忌妒　out of envy

antagonism [æn'tægənɪzəm]

释义· *n.* 对立；对抗；敌意

例句· 好朋友之间也会出现对立。

There is the antagonism among good friends as well.

cautious ['kɔːʃəs]

释义 · *adj.* 谨慎的；小心的

例句 · 他更加谨小慎微，兢兢业业，以尽力取信讨好其上司。

He was even more cautious than ever and did his utmost to win the trust and favor of the superior.

派生 · cautiousness *n.* 谨慎；小心

搭配 · 留心…… ；谨防…… be cautious of

谨慎地做某事 be cautious about doing sth.

mood [muːd]

释义 · *n.* 情绪；心情；坏心境；气氛

例句 · 你必须使自己摆脱这种闷闷不乐的忧郁情绪。

You must rid yourself of this gloomy mood.

搭配 · 糟糕的心情 / 好心情 in a bad/good mood

情绪不好 be in a mood

有意做某事；有做某事的心情 be/feel in the mood for sth.

使某人的情绪好起来 lighten sb.'s mood

compliment ['kɑːmplɪmənt]

释义 · *n.* 称赞；赞扬；恭维

例句 · 一个好的老板会经常称赞他的员工。

A good boss always pays compliments to his or her employees.

搭配 · 称赞某人 pay/give sb. a compliment

把……当作夸奖 take sth. as a compliment

暗含讥讽的恭维，亦夸亦损的话 left-handed compliment

hospitable [hɑːˈspɪtəbl]

释义 · *adj.* 好客的；热情友好的；(环境) 舒适的

例句· 如果你想表现得好客的话，你需要保证客人们总是感觉很舒适。
If you want to be hospitable, you should make sure your guests are always comfortable.

confide [kən'faɪd]

释义· *v.* 吐露（或倾诉）秘密
例句· 好朋友之间可以互相吐露心中的秘密而不用担心隐私。
Good friends can confide in each other without worrying about privacy.
派生· confidential *adj.* 机密的；保密的；受信任的
搭配· 向某人吐露某事　confide sth. to sb.
向（认为可信赖的人）透露秘密（或个人隐私）confide in sb.

eloquent ['eləkwənt]

释义· *adj.* 有说服力的；雄辩的；能言善辩的
例句· 在那次晚宴上，我听到他作了一番非常有说服力的陈词。
I heard him make a very eloquent speech at that dinner.
派生· eloquence *n.* 口才；雄辩

sibling ['sɪblɪŋ]

释义· *n.* 兄弟姐妹
例句· 多数年轻人吸烟都是受朋友或兄弟姐妹的吸烟习惯影响。
Most young smokers are influenced by their friends' and older siblings' smoking habits.
搭配· 兄弟姐妹间的竞争　sibling rivalry

contradictory [ˌkɑːntrə'dɪktəri]

释义· *adj.* 相互矛盾的；对立的；不一致的
例句· 每个人都是一个矛盾的结合体，我们不能绝对地把自己归为某一类人。

Each of us lives a life of contradictory truths. We are not one thing or another.

同根· contradiction *n.* 矛盾；不一致

dynamic [daɪ'næmɪk]

释义· *adj.* 有干劲的；充满活力的；精力充沛的

例句· 他似乎是一个富有干劲、精力充沛的领导。

He seemed a dynamic and energetic leader.

派生· dynamism *n.* 精力；活力；劲头

courteous ['kɜːrtiəs]

释义· *adj.* 有礼貌的；谦恭的

例句· 如果你去一家餐馆，对服务员要有礼貌。

If you go to a restaurant, be courteous to the waiter or waitress.

同根· courtesy *n.* 礼貌；谦恭；彬彬有礼

搭配· 周到的服务 courteous service

intentional [ɪn'tenʃənl]

释义· *adj.* 故意的；有意的；存心的

例句· 受到蓄意歧视的女性将会得到赔偿。

Women who are the victims of intentional discrimination will be able to get compensation.

反义· unintentional *adj.* 无意的；非故意的

搭配· 蓄意犯罪 intentional crime

eternal [ɪ'tɜːrnl]

释义· *adj.* 永恒的；不朽的

例句· 没有永恒的朋友，只有永恒的利益。

There are no eternal friends, only eternal interests.

派生· eternity *n.* 永恒；永远
搭配· 永恒的真理 eternal truth

deceptive [dɪˈseptɪv]

释义· *adj.* 欺骗性的；造成假象的
例句· 外表可能靠不住。
Appearances can be deceptive.
派生· deception *n.* 欺骗
搭配· 欺骗行为 deceptive practices
虚假广告 a deceptive advertisement

modest [ˈmɑːdɪst]

释义· *adj.* 谦虚的；谦逊的；适度的；端庄的
例句· 他一直谦虚谨慎，成名之后仍然如此。
He had always been modest and prudent and remained so after he had become famous.
派生· modesty *n.* 谦逊；质朴

defect [ˈdiːfekt]

释义· *n.* 缺点；缺陷；毛病
例句· 每个人身上都有缺点，我们应该扬长避短，发挥自己的优势。
Everyone has defects, and we should avoid them and take advantage of our strengths.
派生· defective *adj.* 有缺点的；有缺陷的

genuine [ˈdʒenjuɪn]

释义· *adj.* 真诚的；诚实的；可信赖的
例句· 她是我见过的最真诚的人。
She is the most genuine person I've ever met.

chum [tʃʌm]

释义 · *n.* 朋友；友人；伙伴

例句 · 小屋看守人有一个儿子。他是克罗斯杰少爷最要好的朋友之一。

The lodge-keeper had a son who was a chum of Master Grossjay's.

reconcile ['rekənsaɪl]

释义 · *vt.* 使和解；使和谐一致；调和

例句 · 乔纳和他最好的朋友和好了，至少表面上如此。

Jonah and his best friend were, on the surface at least, reconciled.

派生 · reconcilable *adj.* 可和解的；可调和的

搭配 · 使 A 和 B 和解 reconcile sb. with sb.

treacherous ['tretʃərəs]

释义 · *adj.* 背信弃义的；奸诈的；危险的

例句 · 他公开脱离该党，并谴责该党领袖背信弃义。

He publicly left the party and denounced its treacherous leaders.

delight [dɪ'laɪt]

释义 · *n.* 高兴 *vt.* 使高兴；使愉快

例句 · 黑格显然乐于证明他的批评者是错误的。

Haig took obvious delight in proving his critics wrong.

派生 · delightful *adj.* 使人快乐的；令人愉快的；宜人的

搭配 · 以（做）某事为乐（尤指做不该做的事）take delight in (doing) sth.

令某人高兴的是 to sb.'s delight/to the delight of sb.

欣然 with/in delight

contagious [kən'teɪdʒəs]

释义· *adj.* （感情、态度等）感染性的

例句· 安东尼奥对食品赏心悦目这一方面的热情非常有感染性。

Antonio has a contagious enthusiasm for the beautiful aspect of food.

denial [dɪ'naɪəl]

释义· *n.* 拒绝接受；否认；剥夺

例句· 面对人生的重大创痛，例如失去深爱的人，心里的第一反应就是拒绝接受。

With major life traumas, like losing a loved one, for instance, the mind's first reaction is denial.

同根· deniable *adj.* 可否认的；可质疑的

搭配· 否认；拒绝接受现实 in denial

depress [dɪ'pres]

释义· *vt.* 使沮丧；使（经济）不景气；按

例句· 似乎没有人在乎，这让我感到很沮丧。

It depresses me that nobody seems to care.

派生· depressed *adj.* 沮丧的；萧条的

depressing *adj.* 令人抑郁的；令人沮丧的

搭配· 抑制价格 depress price

irrational [ɪ'ræʃənl]

释义· *adj.* 无理性的；不合理的；荒谬的

例句· 如果不明白这之间的差异，那么这个人就是虚伪的、不理性的、没有逻辑的。

If one does not understand the difference, then that person is disingenuous, irrational and illogical.

反义· rational *adj.* 合理的；理性的

派生· irrationality *n.* 不合理

embarrassed [ɪm'bærəst]

释义· *adj.* 尴尬的；窘迫的

例句· 他因自己成为众人注目的中心而感到尴尬。

He felt embarrassed at being the centre of attention.

同根· embarrassment *n.* 窘迫；尴尬；难堪

upbeat ['ʌpbiːt]

释义· *adj.* 乐观的；积极向上的

例句· 非洲人虽生活于最贫穷的大陆，但态度最乐观。

Africans, who live on the poorest continent, were the most upbeat.

emotional [ɪ'moʊʃənl]

释义· *adj.* 情感（上）的；易激动的；感动人的

例句· 在我非常痛苦的时候，她是我的情感支柱。

She provided emotional support at a very distressing time for me.

搭配· 情商 emotional quotient (EQ)

情绪状态 emotional state

情感依恋；情感依附 emotional attachment

irritating ['ɪrɪteɪtɪŋ]

释义· *adj.* 恼人的；使人生气的

例句· 她有打岔的烦人习惯。

She has an irritating habit of interrupting.

同根· irritation *n.* 刺激；生气；恼人事

fantastic [fæn'tæstɪk]

释义· *adj.* 极好的；很大的；怪诞的；不切实际的

例句· 我有着极好的社交生活，朋友多，爱好广。

I have a fantastic social life with many friends and many interests.

搭配· 干得太好了；好样的 fantastic job

solitary ['sɑːləteri]

释义· *adj.* 孤独的；单个的；唯一的

例句· 他终年过着孤独的生活，除忙于园艺之外几乎没有旁的事可做，于是也滋长了好奇心。

Always solitary and busied about his gardening, he had nothing else to do than to indulge his curiosity.

派生· solitude *n.* 独处；独居

faithful ['feɪθfl]

释义· *adj.* 忠实的，忠诚的；如实的；可信任的

例句· 她一直信守承诺，保守着这个秘密。

She had been faithful to her promise to guard this secret.

搭配· 忠实的朋友 a faithful friend

reticent ['retɪsnt]

释义· *adj.* 沉默寡言的；不与人交谈的

例句· 她对自己的成就缄口不言。

She is so reticent about her achievements.

派生· reticence *n.* 沉默寡言

deceitful [dɪ'siːtfl]

释义· *adj.* 欺骗的；欺诈的

例句· 他的态度诡诈而又不老实。

His manner was sly and deceitful.

搭配· 骗术 deceitful trick

虚假新闻 deceitful news

liability [ˌlaɪəˈbɪləti]

释义· *n.* 责任；债务

例句· 他只有 12 岁，所以他不用承担任何责任。

He is only 12 years old, so there's no liability attaching to him.

witty [ˈwɪti]

释义· *adj.* 言辞诙谐的；机智的

例句· 他天性是个爱开玩笑的人，说话诙谐，很有幽默感。

He is, by nature, a joker, a witty man with a sense of fun.

扩展· wittier（比较级）wittiest（最高级）

fascinating [ˈfæsɪneɪtɪŋ]

释义· *adj.* 迷人的；极有吸引力的

例句· 我觉得他很有魅力。

I found him quite fascinating.

同根· fascination *n.* 魅力；入迷

compassionate [kəmˈpæʃənət]

释义· *adj.* 有同情心的；表示怜悯的

例句· 我父亲是一个非常富有同情心的人。

My father was a deeply compassionate man.

piety [ˈpaɪəti]

释义· *n.* (U) 虔诚；虔敬

例句· 弘扬孝道，发扬传统是每个中国人的使命和义务。
Carrying on that tradition and promoting filial piety is the obligation of all Chinese.

搭配· 孝顺；孝心 filial piety

frustrated ['frʌstreɪtɪd]

释义· *adj.* 沮丧的；挫败的

例句· 她对自己的生活感到越来越沮丧。
She had become increasingly frustrated with her life.

同根· frustrating *adj.* 令人沮丧的

glamorous ['glæmərəs]

释义· *adj.* 富有魅力的；迷人的

例句· 她并不迷人，但是她很快乐，因为她的生活压力相对比较少。
She is not glamorous but she's happier because her life is relatively less stressful.

considerate [kən'sɪdərət]

释义· *adj.* 体贴的；考虑周到的

例句· 我觉得他是我所认识的最有魅力并且最为体贴的男士。
I think he's the most charming, most considerate man I've ever known.

搭配· 某人做某事是很体贴的 it is considerate of sb. to do sth.

humble ['hʌmbl]

释义· *adj.* 卑微的；谦逊的 *vt.* 贬低

例句· 亚科卡出身卑微，后来成了福特公司的总裁。
Iacocca rose from humble beginnings to become boss of Ford.

搭配· 承认错误；赔礼道歉 eat humble pie

作出谦恭的姿态 humble yourself

扩展· humbler（比较级）humblest（最高级）

indolent ['ɪndələnt]

释义· *adj.* 懒惰的；懒散的

例句· 他不学无术又好逸恶劳，成功的前景微乎甚微。

He is ignorant and indolent, which makes the prospects of his success greyer than grey.

派生· indolence *n.* 懒散；懒惰

articulate [ɑːrˈtɪkjuleɪt]

释义· *adj.* 善于表达的；口齿伶俐的 *v.* 明确表达；清晰发（音）

例句· 她是一个口才很好的年轻女子。

She is an articulate young woman.

irresponsible [ˌɪrɪˈspɑːnsəbl]

释义· *adj.* 不负责任的；无责任感的

例句· 他把孩子们独自留在游泳池里，真是太不负责任了。

It was highly irresponsible of him to leave the children on their own in the pool.

搭配· （某人）做某事是不负责任的 it is irresponsible (of sb.) to do sth.

不负责任的言论 irresponsible remarks

extroverted ['ekstrəvɜːrtɪd]

释义· *adj.* 活泼友好的；外向的

例句· 一些年轻人孩童时脾气随和、性格活泼，刚进入青春期却变得害羞起来。

Some young people who were easy-going and extroverted as children become self-conscious in early adolescence.

反义· introverted *adj.* 内向的

nonsense ['nɑ:nsens]

释义· *n.* 胡说；假话；愚蠢的话
例句· 在严肃的外交场合你可不能唠唠叨叨地胡说一气。
You mustn't chatter nonsense on serious diplomatic occasions.
搭配· 做某事很荒谬　it is (a) nonsense to do sth.
一派胡言　sheer nonsense

impetuous [ɪm'petʃuəs]

释义· *adj.* 鲁莽的；冲动的
例句· 他情绪高昂，行事鲁莽。
He was high-spirited and impetuous.
派生· impetuosity *n.* 急性；冲动

thoughtful ['θɔ:tfl]

释义· *adj.* 深思的；体贴的；考虑周到的
例句· 毫无疑问，盖茨部长是一个深思熟虑的人，一个伟大的管理者和一个良好的政治家。
There is no question that Secretary Gates is a thoughtful man, a great administrator and a good politician.
搭配· 某人做某事是周到的　it is thoughtful of sb. to do sth.
体贴入微的关照；考虑周到　thoughtful consideration

devious ['di:viəs]

释义· *adj.* 阴险的；奸诈的；狡猾的；迂回的
例句· 纽曼阴险得很，明里一套，暗里一套。
Newman was devious, prepared to say one thing in print and another in private.

nostalgia [nə'stældʒə]

释义· *n.* (U) 怀旧；念旧

例句· 她对自己的大学时代充满了怀念之情。

She is filled with nostalgia for her own college days.

派生· nostalgic *adj.* 怀旧的；恋旧的

搭配· 对美好过去的留恋 nostalgia for the good old days

amusing [ə'mjuːzɪŋ]

释义· *adj.* 逗人笑的；有乐趣的；好笑的

例句· 他极具幽默感，很会逗人发笑。

He had a terrific sense of humor and could be very amusing.

notorious [nəʊ'tɔːriəs]

释义· *adj.* 臭名昭著的；声名狼藉的

例句· 这名法官已为一些最臭名昭著的罪犯当过辩护律师。

The lawyer has defended some of the most notorious criminals.

派生· notoriety *n.* 恶名；坏名声

passive ['pæsɪv]

释义· *adj.* 被动的；消极的；顺从的

例句· 凯茜在这一关系中似乎扮演着十分被动的角色。

Kathy seems to take a very passive role in the relationship.

搭配· 吸二手烟 passive smoking

grateful ['greɪtfl]

释义· *adj.* 感激的；表示感谢的

例句· 我非常感激能在大学里拿到这样一份工作，能让我同时做好这些事情。

I'm grateful to have a job at a college that enables me to do all this.

反义· ungrateful *adj.* 忘恩负义的；不领情的

派生· gratefulness *n.* 感激；感恩

picky ['pɪki]

释义· *adj.* 挑剔的；难伺候的

例句· 有些人对选择跟什么样的人共享生活非常挑剔。

Some people are very picky about who they choose to share their lives with.

搭配· 挑食者　picky-eater

挑剔的顾客　picky customer

propensity [prə'pensəti]

释义· *n.* 倾向；习性

例句· 宾特先生习惯拖到最后时刻才作决定。

Mr. Bint has a propensity to put off decisions to the last minute.

搭配· 有做某事的倾向　propensity to do sth.

消费倾向　propensity to consume

reckless ['rekləs]

释义· *adj.* 鲁莽的，不计后果的

例句· 他对他们的鲁莽行为道了歉。

He apologized for their reckless behavior.

派生· recklessness *n.* 鲁莽；轻率

搭配· 鲁莽驾驶　reckless driving

轻率的行为　reckless conduct

ridiculous [rɪ'dɪkjələs]

释义· *adj.* 可笑的；荒谬的；愚蠢的

例句· 她突然插嘴提了个可笑的异议。

She broke in with a ridiculous objection.

搭配· 胡思乱想；荒谬的想法 ridiculous thoughts

sagacious [sə'geɪʃəs]

释义· *adj.* 睿智的；聪慧的

例句· 我的伯父是一个非常睿智和幽默的人，像一个哲学家。

My uncle is a very sagacious and humorous person who is more like a philosopher.

派生· sagacity *n.* 聪慧；精明；有决策力

keen [ki:n]

释义· *adj.* 思维敏捷的；机灵的；渴望的；强烈的

例句· 他们把他描述成一个才思敏捷的人。

They described him as a man of keen intellect.

搭配· 渴望做某事 be keen to do sth./ keen on doing sth.

喜欢某人 / 某物 be keen on sb./sth.

激烈的竞争 keen competition

浓厚的兴趣 keen interest

satisfied ['sætɪsfaɪd]

释义· *adj.* 满足的；满意的

例句· 她对自己的所得贪得无厌。

She's never satisfied with what she's got.

同根· satisfying *adj.* 令人满意（或满足）的

satisfaction *n.* 满意；满足

搭配· 对……感到满意 be satisfied with sth.

gregarious [grɪˈgeriəs]

释义 · *adj.* 爱交际的；合群的
例句 · 她很外向，喜欢交朋结友。
She is such a gregarious and outgoing person.

rebellious [rɪˈbeljəs]

释义 · *adj.* 叛逆的；反叛的
例句 · 不少受害者都是叛逆的少女，她们经常离家出走，和父母素有矛盾，或者触犯法规。
Many of the victims are rebellious teenage girls—often runaways—who have been in trouble with their parents and the law.
同根 · rebellion *n.* 叛乱；反抗

predictable [prɪˈdɪktəbl]

释义 · *adj.* 老套乏味的；意料之中的；可预见的
例句 · 他为人很不错，但我觉得他相当呆板乏味。
He is very nice, but I find him rather dull and predictable.
反义 · unpredictable *adj.* （人）善变的，难以捉摸的；不可预测的

exclusive [ɪkˈskluːsɪv]

释义 · *adj.* 排斥的；独有的；排外的；高级的
例句 · 他们都明白了事业心与做个成功的父亲是互相排斥的。
They both have learned that ambition and successful fatherhood can be mutually exclusive.
派生 · exclusiveness *n.* 排他性；独占
搭配 · 不包括某人 / 某物　exclusive of sb./sth.
独家新闻　exclusive news

skeptical ['skeptɪkl]

释义· *adj.* 怀疑的

例句· 他对爱情和浪漫持非常怀疑的态度。

He takes a rather skeptical view of love and romance.

搭配· 怀疑性思维 skeptical thinking

极度怀疑 highly/deeply skeptical

descendant [dɪ'sendənt]

释义· *n.* 子孙；后裔

例句· 但是他没有忘记自己是炎黄子孙，对祖国始终充满了爱。

However, he never forgot that he was a Chinese descendant and he cherished a deep love for his country.

搭配· 炎黄子孙 Chinese descendant

suspicious [sə'spɪʃəs]

释义· *adj.* 怀疑的；猜疑的；可疑的

例句· 他的一些同事开始怀疑他的行为。

Some of his colleagues at work became suspicious of his behavior.

搭配· 对……起疑 be suspicious of/about sth.

hilarious [hɪ'leriəs]

释义· *adj.* 引人捧腹大笑的；滑稽的；极有趣的

例句· 我们第一次听说此事时，觉得很好笑。

We thought it was hilarious when we first heard about it.

sympathetic [ˌsɪmpə'θetɪk]

释义· *adj.* 同情的；赞同的；合意的

例句· 我很同情那些家长，他们都很担心自己的孩子所看的电视内容。

I'm sympathetic to parents who are worried about what their children see on television.

同根· sympathize *v.* 同情；赞同；支持

egocentric [ˌiːɡoʊˈsentrɪk]

释义· *adj.* 以自我为中心的；自私自利的

例句· 他是个以自我为中心、易冲动的人，希望身边的人都为他服务。
He was egocentric, a man of impulse who expected those around him to serve him.

trustworthy [ˈtrʌstwɜːrði]

释义· *adj.* 可信赖的；可靠的

例句· 他是个头脑冷静、值得信赖的领导。
He is a trustworthy and level-headed leader.

反义· untrustworthy *adj.* 不可信的；不可靠的

搭配· 信得过产品 trustworthy product

indifferent [ɪnˈdɪfrənt]

释义· *adj.* 不关心的；不感兴趣的；冷淡的

例句· 人们对别人的痛苦已经变得无动于衷。
People have become indifferent to the suffering of others.

派生· indifference *n.* 不感兴趣；漠不关心

搭配· 冷遇 indifferent treatment

unwilling [ʌnˈwɪlɪŋ]

释义· *adj.* 不情愿的；不愿意的

例句· 作为一名年轻教师，他发现自己被迫参与到了学校的权力争斗中。
A youthful teacher, he finds himself an unwilling participant in school politics.

反义· willing *adj.* 乐意的；愿意的

搭配· 不愿意做某事 be unwilling to do sth.

cohort [ˈkoʊhɔːrt]

释义· *n.* 朋友；支持者；助手

例句· 德雷克那一帮人对我的任命很不满。

Drake and his cohorts were not pleased with my appointment.

常 用 短 语

释义	短语
患难之交	a tested friend/a friend in need/adversity
终身好友	a lifelong friend
靠不住的朋友；酒肉朋友	fair-weather friend
使某人接触某物	expose sb. to sth.
低调的	low-profile/low-key
个人活动	solitary activity
家庭观念	family values
单亲家庭	single-parent households
闲逛	hang out
了解近况；叙旧	catch up
过去的美好时光	the good old days
狭隘的生活态度	a parochial outlook toward life
后见之明	with hindsight
代沟	generation gap
挥之不去	linger in one's mind
回顾	in retrospect
让某人逐渐放得开	bring a person out of his/her shell
体弱的	physically weak

预期寿命；平均（期望）寿命	life expectancy
传统心态	traditional mentality
不同的世界观	different world outlook
根深蒂固的	deep-seated/inveterate
某事物并不是一成不变的	be not curved in stone
依恋感	a sense of attachment
情感依恋	emotional attachment
子女义务；孝	filial duties
老龄化社会	aging society
照顾老人	take care of the elderly
"空巢"综合症	empty-nest syndrome
家务活儿	household chores
核心家庭，小家庭（只包括父母和子女）	nuclear family
某人的亲戚	one's relatives

巩固练习

练习1 根据下面的中文释义，写出对应的单词（词组）。

A

可信赖的 t＿＿＿＿＿

睿智的 s＿＿＿＿＿

同情的 s＿＿＿＿＿

缺点 d＿＿＿＿＿

性格 t＿＿＿＿＿

责任 l＿＿＿＿＿

孤独的 s＿＿＿＿＿

叙旧 c＿＿＿＿＿

老龄化社会 a＿＿＿＿＿

外向的 e＿＿＿＿＿

相互的 m＿＿＿＿＿

B

鲁莽的 i＿＿＿＿＿

代沟 g＿＿＿＿＿

机敏的 a＿＿＿＿＿

真诚的 s＿＿＿＿＿

有条理的 o＿＿＿＿＿

不同的世界观 d＿＿＿＿＿

低调的 l＿＿＿＿＿

辜负 b＿＿＿＿＿

高雅的 e＿＿＿＿＿

有礼貌的 c＿＿＿＿＿

患难之交 a＿＿＿＿＿

练习2 用方框中所给单词（词组）的适当形式填空。

confide in	absurd	fantastic	frustrated
appreciate	notorious	dynamic	depress
suspicious of	bewilder	indifferent	satisfied with
sympathetic	considerate	hesitant about	

1. It's a＿＿＿＿＿（荒谬的）to suggest that they knew what was going on but did nothing.

2. Peter stood by me when I most needed it. I'll always a＿＿＿＿（感激）that.

3. Wealth cannot b＿＿＿＿（使迷惑）one's mind, poverty cannot undermine one's moral integrity, and force cannot seize one's dignity.

4. She was h＿＿＿＿（对……犹豫）coming forward with her story.

5. Good friends can c＿＿＿＿（吐露秘密）each other without worrying about privacy.

6. He seemed a d＿＿＿＿（有干劲的）and energetic leader.

7. It d＿＿＿＿（使沮丧）me that nobody seems to care.

8. I have a f＿＿＿＿（极好的）social life with many friends and many interests.

9. She had become increasingly f＿＿＿＿（沮丧的）with her life.

10. I think he's the most charming, most c＿＿＿＿（体贴的）man I've ever known.

11. The lawyer has defended some of the most n＿＿＿＿（臭名昭著的）criminals.

12. She's never s＿＿＿＿（满足）what she's got.

13. Some of his colleagues at work became s＿＿＿＿（怀疑）his behavior.

14. I'm s＿＿＿＿（同情的）to parents who are worried about what their children see on television.

15. People have become i＿＿＿＿（不关心的）to the suffering of others.

- [ ] sociable
- [ ] abnormal
- [ ] loyalty
- [ ] absurd
- [ ] cooperative
- [ ] affection
- [ ] betray
- [ ] organized
- [ ] appreciate
- [ ] vain
- [ ] arbitrary
- [ ] mutual
- [ ] temperament
- [ ] astute
- [ ] awkward
- [ ] congenial
- [ ] sincere
- [ ] bewilder
- [ ] spouse
- [ ] candid
- [ ] baffle
- [ ] hesitant
- [ ] contemptuous
- [ ] greed

- [ ] elegant
- [ ] casual
- [ ] envy
- [ ] antagonism
- [ ] cautious
- [ ] mood
- [ ] compliment
- [ ] hospitable
- [ ] confide
- [ ] eloquent
- [ ] sibling
- [ ] contradictory
- [ ] dynamic
- [ ] courteous
- [ ] intentional
- [ ] eternal
- [ ] deceptive
- [ ] modest
- [ ] defect
- [ ] genuine
- [ ] chum
- [ ] reconcile
- [ ] treacherous
- [ ] delight

- [ ] contagious
- [ ] denial
- [ ] depress
- [ ] irrational
- [ ] embarrassed
- [ ] upbeat
- [ ] emotional
- [ ] irritating
- [ ] fantastic
- [ ] solitary
- [ ] faithful
- [ ] reticent
- [ ] deceitful
- [ ] liability
- [ ] witty
- [ ] fascinating
- [ ] compassionate
- [ ] piety
- [ ] frustrated
- [ ] glamorous
- [ ] considerate
- [ ] humble
- [ ] indolent
- [ ] articulate

□ irresponsible	□ propensity	□ suspicious
□ extroverted	□ reckless	□ hilarious
□ nonsense	□ ridiculous	□ sympathetic
□ impetuous	□ sagacious	□ egocentric
□ thoughtful	□ keen	□ trustworthy
□ devious	□ satisfied	□ indifferent
□ nostalgia	□ gregarious	□ unwilling
□ amusing	□ rebellious	□ cohort
□ notorious	□ predictable	
□ passive	□ exclusive	
□ grateful	□ skeptical	
□ picky	□ descendant	

表中共有 104 个单词

您不确认的单词 _____ 个，占总数的 _____%

如果比例高于 10%，请耐心再复习一遍。如果比例低于 10%，您可以开始下一章的托福写作之旅了！

生态环境

pollutant [pə'luːtənt]

释义· *n.* 污染物；污染物质

例句· 工业污染物会引发多种癌症。

Industrial pollutants are responsible for a sizable proportion of all cancers.

同根· pollution *n.* 污染

搭配· 污染物排放 pollutant discharge

污染源 pollutant source

化学污染物 chemical pollutant

recycle [ˌriː'saɪkl]

释义· *v.* 回收利用；再利用

例句· 我们把所有的瓶子都回收利用起来。

We take all our bottles to be recycled.

派生· recyclable *adj.* 可回收利用的

primitive ['prɪmətɪv]

释义· *adj.* 原始的；远古的；简陋的

例句· 原始的游牧部落与自然和谐相处。

The primitive nomadic tribe live in harmony with nature.

派生· primitively *adv.* 最初地

adapt [ə'dæpt]

释义· *v.* （使）适应；（使）适合；改编

例句· 这些昆虫是如何适应新环境的？

How do these insects adapt themselves to new environments?

派生· adaptable *adj.* 能适应的；适应性强的

adaptive *adj.* 适应的；有适应能力的

搭配· 适应新情况 adapt to

为……改编 adapt for/from

hostile ['hɑːstl]

释义· *adj.* （生存环境）恶劣的，不利的；敌对的

例句· 世界上最恶劣的几种气候条件分别是什么？

What are the most hostile climatic conditions in the world?

派生· hostility *n.* 敌意；敌对行为

搭配· 不利的环境；恶劣的环境 hostile conditions

groundless ['graʊndləs]

释义· *adj.* 无根据的；无理由的

例句· 事实证明没有证据表明全世界的能源将会枯竭。

Fears that the world was about to run out of fuel proved groundless.

dump [dʌmp]

释义· *v.* 丢弃；扔掉；乱扔 *n.* 垃圾场

例句· 太多的有毒废料在向大海里倾倒。

Too much toxic waste is being dumped at sea.

搭配· 把（某事）推给他人负责 dump/drop sth. in sb.'s lap

minimize ['mɪnɪmaɪz]

释义· *v.* 使减少到最低限度；降低；贬低

例句· 但这也同样意味着日本拥有资源尽量减少损失。

But it also means that Japan has the resources to minimize the damage.

反义· maximize *v.* 使增加到最大限度；充分利用

同根· minimal *adj.* 最小的；最低限度的

foul [faʊl]

释义· *adj.* 肮脏的；难闻的 *v.* 弄脏；对……犯规 *n.* 犯规

例句· 发生在洛杉矶附近的两起漏油事故已经污染了那里的海洋和天空。

Two oil-related accidents near Los Angeles have fouled the ocean and the skies there.

搭配· 大量出错；搞糟 foul up

污水 foul water

脏话 foul language

扩展· fouler（比较级）foulest（最高级）

conserve [kən'sɜːrv]

释义· *vt.* 保护；保存；节约

例句· 我们必须为子孙后代保护林地。

We must conserve our woodlands for future generations.

派生· conservation *n.* 保护

搭配· 节约能源 conserve energy

decline [dɪˈklaɪn]

释义· *n.* 减少；下降；衰退 *v.* 减少；下降；谢绝

例句· 汽车的增加导致了公共交通的减少。

An increase in cars has resulted in the decline of public transport.

派生· declination *n.* 衰退；倾斜；偏差

搭配· 拒绝做某事 decline to do sth.

在低落中；在衰退中 on the decline

衰亡；衰败 decline and fall

adjustment [əˈdʒʌstmənt]

释义· *n.* 调整；调节

例句· 我已对设计作了几处调整。

I've made a few adjustments to the design.

同根· adjustable *adj.* 可调整的；可调节的

exceed [ɪkˈsiːd]

释义· *v.* 超过；超出

例句· 现在的污染速度已经超过了环境的承载能力。

Now the pollution rate has exceeded the carrying capacity of the environment.

convert [kənˈvɜːrt]

释义· *v.* （使）转变，转换，转化

例句· 他决定把这片沙漠变成绿洲。

He decided to convert the desert into the oasis.

派生· convertible *adj.* 可转换的；可改变的

搭配· （使）A 转变成 B　convert sth. to/into sth.

mine [maɪn]

释义· *v.* 开采；采矿 *n.* 矿

例句· 这座煤矿即将关闭，因为从经济上考虑，矿井里已经没有足够的煤可供开采。

The pit is being shut down because it no longer has enough coal that can be mined economically.

派生· mineral *n.* 矿物；矿物质

搭配· （关于某人 / 某物的）信息源泉；知识宝库　a mine of information (about/on sb./sth.)

restore [rɪ'stɔːr]

释义· *v.* 恢复；修复；使复原

例句· 环保组织想尽力把这片森林恢复到原来的状态。

Environmental groups want to try to restore the forest to its former state.

派生· restoration *n.* 修复；恢复

搭配· 把 A 恢复到 B　restore sth. to sth.

posterity [pɑː'sterəti]

释义· *n.* (U) 子孙；后代；后裔

例句· 为了我们的国家、民族和子孙后代，我们需要立刻保护环境。

For the sake of our country, our nation and our posterity, we need to protect the environment immediately.

chronic ['krɑːnɪk]

释义· *adj.* 慢性的；长期的

例句· 有些慢性病跟环境污染有紧密关系。

Some chronic diseases are closely related to environmental

pollution.

搭配· 慢性病 chronic disease

该国长期存在的失业问题 the country's chronic unemployment problem

inhabit [ɪn'hæbɪt]

释义· *v.* 栖居于；居住于

例句· 啄木鸟栖息在中空的树中。

Woodpeckers inhabit hollow trees.

派生· inhabitant *n.* （某地的）居民，栖息动物

pointlessly ['pɔɪntləsli]

释义· *adv.* 无谓地

例句· 化学品在无谓地污染着土壤。

Chemicals were pointlessly poisoning the soil.

endanger [ɪn'deɪndʒər]

释义· *vt.* 使遭危险；危及；危害

例句· 我们孩子们的健康正受到排放出的废气的损害。

The health of our children is being endangered by exhaust fumes.

派生· endangered *adj.* 濒临灭绝的；有生命危险的

endangerment *n.* 危害

disgrace [dɪs'greɪs]

释义· *n.* 耻辱；丢脸 *vt.* 使丢脸；使蒙受耻辱

例句· 为了自己的利益而伤害甚至毁灭其他物种，这对人类来说简直是耻辱。

It would be a disgrace for human beings to harm, and even destroy other species for their own sake.

派生· disgraceful *adj.* 可耻的；丢脸的

搭配· 通过做某事使自己蒙羞 disgrace yourself by doing sth.

丢脸；不光彩 in disgrace

culprit ['kʌlprɪt]

释义· *n.* 引起问题的事物；罪犯

例句· 但过量使用某个种类的氮肥是另一个原因，这恰恰是研究者最为肯定使得中国耕地酸化的罪魁祸首。

But overuse of certain types of nitrogen fertilizer is another cause, and this is what the researchers identify as the culprit in China.

irrigation [ˌɪrɪ'geɪʃn]

释义· *n.* 灌溉

例句· 中国部分地区水污染程度之重，甚至达到不能接触的程度，更不用说用于灌溉或者饮用。

Its water is so contaminated that in some areas it is unsafe even to touch, let alone use for irrigation or drinking.

remedial [rɪ'miːdiəl]

释义· *adj.* 补救的；纠正的

例句· 一些权威机构现在不得不采取补救行动来拯救濒危物种。

Some authorities are now having to take remedial action to save the endangered species.

搭配· 补救措施 remedial measure

ecosystem ['iːkoʊsɪstəm]

释义· *n.* 生态系统

例句· 通过我的照片我想让人们明白，如果我们失去了海冰，我们就会失去整个生态系统。

And with my photography I want people to understand that if we lose ice, we stand to lose an entire ecosystem.

搭配· 生态多样性 ecosystem diversity

crude [kruːd]

释义· *adj.* 天然的；自然的；简略的；粗糙的
例句· 1000 吨原油从一艘油轮中泄漏，流入了海洋。
A thousand tons of crude oil has spilled into the sea from an oil tanker.

搭配· 简单地说 in crude terms

shortage ['ʃɔːrtɪdʒ]

释义· *n.* 缺乏；缺少；不足
例句· 这个国家的水资源匮乏可能会带来灾难性的后果。
The water shortage in this country is potentially catastrophic.

搭配· 缺乏某物 the shortage of sth.
用水短缺 water shortages
电力短缺 power shortage

scarcity ['skersəti]

释义· *n.* 缺乏；不足；稀少
例句· 如果我们没有这样做，这里很快会变成一个缺乏资源的世界。
If we do not, it rapidly becomes a world of scarcity.

disastrous [dɪ'zæstrəs]

释义· *adj.* 灾难性的；完全失败的
例句· 气候变化可能给地球带来灾难性的影响。
Climate change could have disastrous effects on Earth.

搭配· 灾难性后果 disastrous consequences

扩展	释义	单词	释义	单词
	灾难	disaster	悲剧	tragedy
	灾祸	calamity	重大灾难	catastrophe

toxic ['tɑ:ksɪk]

释义· *adj.* 有毒的；引起中毒的

例句· 有毒废物可能危及生命，毒死鱼类。

Toxic waste could endanger lives and poison fish.

派生· toxicity *n.* 毒性

搭配· 有毒的物质　toxic substance

poisonous ['pɔɪzənəs]

释义· *adj.* 有毒的；令人厌恶的

例句· 那个化工厂排出大量有毒的废水。

A lot of poisonous waste water comes from that chemical factory.

搭配· 有毒的物质　poisonous substance

barbaric [bɑ:r'bærɪk]

释义· *adj.* 野蛮的；凶残的

例句· 对鲸的野蛮宰杀既不必要也不人道。

The barbaric slaughter of whales is unnecessary and inhuman.

同根· barbarian *n.* 野蛮人

barbarity *n.* 暴行；残忍

cruel ['kru:əl]

释义· *adj.* 残忍的；残酷的；冷酷的

例句· 我无法容忍虐待动物的人。

I can't stand people who are cruel to animals.

派生· cruelty *n.* 残忍；残暴；残酷的行为

搭配· 良药苦口 be cruel to be kind

origin [ˈɔːrɪdʒɪn]

释义· *n.* 起源；起因；出身

例句· 达尔文对许多事实加以归纳，得出了他对于人类起源的看法。

Darwin generalized from many facts to reach his idea about the origin of man.

派生· originate *v.* 发源；来自；创始

original *adj.* 原来的；独创的 *n.* 原作

搭配· 卑微的出身 humble origin

原产地；原产国 country of origin

起源于 in origin

filter [ˈfɪltər]

释义· *v.* 过滤；渗透；慢慢传开 *n.* 过滤器

例句· 臭氧层过滤掉有害的太阳紫外线。

The ozone layer filters harmful UV rays from the sun.

搭配· 空气过滤器 air filter

过滤掉 filter out

supply [səˈplaɪ]

释义· *n.* 供应；供给；储备 *v.* 供应，供给

例句· 可开发利用的原材料供应不足。

Exploitable raw materials were in short supply.

搭配· 向某人提供某物 supply sb. with sth./supply sth. to sb.

供应不足；缺乏 in short supply

食物供给 food supply

distaste [dɪsˈteɪst]

释义· *n.* 厌恶；不喜欢；反感

例句· 他厌恶地环顾着这肮脏的房间。

He looked around the filthy room in distaste.

派生· distasteful *adj.* 使人不愉快的；令人反感的

搭配· 厌恶某人 / 某物　distaste for sb./sth.

purify [ˈpjʊrɪfaɪ]

释义· *v.* 净化；使纯净

例句· 风力发电机和太阳能电池可以产生电能，雨水收集系统能够收集并净化雨水。

Wind turbines and solar cells will generate electricity and a rainwater collection system will harvest and purify rain.

派生· purification *n.* 净化；提纯

contribute [kənˈtrɪbjuːt]

释义· *v.* （为⋯⋯）做贡献；捐献；促成

例句· 我相信我们每一个人都能为世界环境的改善做出贡献。

I believe that each of us can contribute to the improvement of the world environment.

派生· contribution *n.* 贡献；投稿

搭配· 是某事的原因之一　contribute to sth.

把⋯⋯捐献给⋯⋯　contribute sth. to/towards sth.

torture [ˈtɔːrtʃər]

释义· *n.* 折磨；拷问 *v.* 虐待；拷打

例句· 他们通过折磨、囚禁和残酷对待无数动物来获利，并设法隐藏这些行为。

They have profited off of the torture, confinement, and cruel

treatment of countless animals, and actively hide these practices.

派生· torturous *adj.* 折磨人的；极端痛苦的

ruin ['ruːɪn]

释义· *v.* 毁坏；毁灭；使破产 *n.* 废墟；毁坏；破产

例句· 人类毁坏了许多动物的家园，破坏了许多原生态的环境。
Human ruined many animal's homes and destroyed many original ecological environments.

派生· ruinous *adj.* 破坏性的；毁灭性的

搭配· 毁坏；严重受损 in ruins
经济损失 financial ruin
砸牌子；损坏名誉 ruin reputation

subject [səb'dʒekt]

释义· *v.* 使遭受；使经受

例句· 海洋受到了人类的严重破坏，比如石油泄漏和过度捕捞。
Oceans are subjected to significant damage from humans, such as oil spills and overfishing.

派生· subjection *n.* 隶属；服从

inhale [ɪn'heɪl]

释义· *v.* 吸入；吸气

例句· 他因吸入烟尘而接受治疗。
He was treated for the effects of inhaling smoke.

派生· inhalation *n.* 吸入

deforestation [ˌdiːˌfɔːrɪ'steɪʃn]

释义· *n.* (U) 滥伐树林；毁林

例句· 森林砍伐还能改变土壤状态，加剧土壤侵蚀，这两者都能把更多的碳释放到大气中。

Deforestation can also change soil dynamics and increase erosion, both of which can release more carbon into the atmosphere.

irreversible [ˌɪrɪ'vɜːrsəbl]

释义· *adj.* 不可逆转的；不可挽回的

例句· 化石燃料已对环境造成了不可逆转的破坏。

Fossil fuels have caused irreversible damage to the environment.

dearth [dɜːrθ]

释义· *n.* 缺乏；不足

例句· 如果再考虑到被污染的淡水总量，我们便处于缺乏安全且可饮用水源的境地中。

If you then factor in the amount of contaminated and polluted fresh water, we are left with a dearth of safe, drinkable water.

contaminate [kən'tæmɪneɪt]

释义· *vt.* 污染；弄脏

例句· 饮用水被铅污染了。

The drinking water has become contaminated with lead.

派生· contaminated *adj.* 被污染的

contamination *n.* 污染

reclaim [rɪ'kleɪm]

释义· *v.* 开垦；利用；改造；收回

例句· 荷兰人一直在围海造地。

The Netherlands has been reclaiming farmland from water.

搭配· 被开发利用的沼泽地 reclaimed marshland

emission [i'mɪʃn]

释义· *n.*（光、热等）排放，发出；散出

例句· 二氧化碳等气体的排放应该被控制在目前的水平上。

The emission of gases such as carbon dioxide should be stabilized at their present level.

搭配· 减少排放 emission reduction

unwarranted [ʌn'wɔːrəntɪd]

释义· *adj.* 无正当理由的

例句· 人类为了自己的生存而屠杀其他动物是毫无道理可言的。

It is unwarranted that humans kill other animals for their survival.

搭配· 无理干涉 unwarranted interference

不当的要求 unwarranted demand

fumes [fjuːmz]

释义· *n.*（浓烈的或有害的）烟，气，汽

例句· 汽车尾气中的某些物质会增加空气污染，危害人体健康。

Some substances in automobile exhaust fumes can increase air pollution and harm human health.

搭配· 汽车尾气 car exhaust fumes

outweigh [ˌaʊt'weɪ]

释义· *vt.* 大于；超过；重于

例句· 有些人可能认为采取一些行动来治理环境会花费很多，但是这些行动的好处远远大于投入。

Some people may think that taking some actions to clean the environment will cost a lot, but the benefits of such actions far outweigh the costs.

搭配· 远大于 far outweigh

利大于弊 benefits outweigh the disadvantages

利益大于一切 benefits outweigh all

mirror ['mɪrər]

释义· *vt.* 反映；反射 *n.* 镜子

例句· 常年的雾霾反映了这座城市糟糕的空气质量。

The perennial haze mirrors the city's poor air quality.

搭配· 反映某事物的一面镜子 a mirror of sth.

镜像 mirror image

evolution [ˌiːvəˈluːʃn]

释义· *n.* (U) 进化；演变

例句· 如果进化论是讲适者生存，在弱肉强食的自然界，动物怎么能进化出道德情感？

If evolution is survival of the fittest, nature red in tooth and claw, how could animals evolve moral feelings?

派生· evolutionary *adj.* 进化的；演变的

搭配· 进化论 the theory of evolution

社会进化 social evolution

alter ['ɔːltər]

释义· *v.* （使）改变，更改

例句· 地貌已被彻底改变，这严重危及了野生生物。

The landscape has been radically altered, severely damaging wildlife.

派生· alteration *n.* 改变；改动

搭配· 密友，至交 alter ego

equilibrium [ˌiːkwɪˈlɪbriəm]

释义· *n.* 平衡；平静

例句· 对身体平衡状态的任何干扰都可能产生压力。

Any disturbance to the body's state of equilibrium can produce stress.

搭配· 生态平衡 ecological equilibrium

infertile [ɪnˈfɜːrtl]

释义· *adj.* 贫瘠的；不肥沃的；不育的

例句· 这片土地荒芜而贫瘠。

The land was barren and infertile.

派生· infertility *n.* 贫瘠；不孕

dissipate [ˈdɪsɪpeɪt]

释义· *v.* （使）消失，消散；浪费

例句· 辐射量会随着离核电站的距离渐远而快速消失。

That dose of radiation would quickly dissipate with distance from the plant.

派生· dissipated *adj.* 放荡的；花天酒地的

搭配· 消除疲劳 dissipate fatigue

smog [smɑːg]

释义· *n.* 烟雾

例句· 城市上空罩上了一层浓雾。

The sky over the city was overspread with a layer of heavy smog.

派生· smoggy *adj.* 烟雾弥漫的

搭配· 光化雾 photochemical smog

decompose [ˌdiːkəmˈpoʊz]

释义· v. （使）腐烂；（使）分解

例句· 废物腐烂时会产生沼气。

As the waste materials decompose, they produce methane gas.

派生· decomposition n. 分解；腐烂

搭配· 使 A 分解为 B decompose sth. into sth.

gradually [ˈɡrædʒuəli]

释义· adv. 逐步地；逐渐地

例句· 附近的工厂每天晚上都在排放有毒的气体，以至于当地人渐渐地闻到了一股难闻的气味。

Nearby factories are emitting poisonous gases every night so that local people gradually became aware of an awful smell.

lessen [ˈlesn]

释义· v. （使）减轻；（使）减少

例句· 这个新项目将减轻汽车污染的影响。

The new project will lessen the effects of car pollution.

搭配· 减轻负担 lessen burden

减少某事物的风险 / 影响 / 效果 lessen the risk/impact/effect of sth.

sensitive [ˈsensətɪv]

释义· adj. 易受影响的；敏感的；体贴的

例句· 湿地是容易受环境影响的区域。

Wetlands are environmentally sensitive areas.

反义· insensitive adj. 不敏感的；感觉迟钝的

同根 · sensitivity *n.* 敏感；体贴

搭配 · 对某物敏感的 be sensitive to sth.

cripple ['krɪpl]

释义 · *vt.* 严重毁坏（或损害）；使残废 *n.* 跛子；残疾人

例句 · 石棉纤维会破坏肺组织，留下损伤，削弱器官的氧气处理机能，有时还会引发肺癌。

Asbestos fibers can bruise the lung tissue, leaving scars that cripple the organ's ability to process oxygen and sometimes cause lung cancer.

派生 · crippling *adj.* （疾病等）严重损害健康（或身体）的

搭配 · 感情有缺陷者（指无法向别人表达自己感情的人）emotional cripple

penetrate ['penətreɪt]

释义 · *v.* 穿过；渗透；洞察；看透

例句 · 水是世界上最柔软的物质，但是它却可以穿透最坚硬的岩石，比如花岗岩等石材。

Water is the softest substance in the world, but yet it can penetrate the hardest rock or anything—granite, you name it.

派生 · penetrating *adj.* 锐利的；渗透的

penetration *n.* 渗透

搭配 · 穿过某物 penetrate into/through/to sth.

severe [sɪ'vɪr]

释义 · *adj.* 十分严重的；极为恶劣的；严厉的

例句 · 这场暴风雨造成了严重的破坏。

The storm caused severe damage.

派生· severity *n.* 严重；严格

搭配· 恶劣的天气 severe weather

　　　　严寒 severe cold

questionable ['kwestʃənəbl]

释义· *adj.* 有问题的；可疑的

例句· 政府正在进行的大规模填海造地行为是值得商榷的。

　　　　It is questionable that the government are conducting massive land-reclamation.

搭配· 疑点 questionable point

　　　　可疑行为 questionable conduct

sewage ['suːɪdʒ]

释义· *n.* (U)（下水道的）污水，污物

例句· 这些化学品渗入污水系统，最终可能进入我们的饮用水中。

　　　　Those chemicals pass through the sewage system and might even end up in our drinking water.

搭配· 污水处理 sewage disposal

　　　　工业废水 industrial sewage

　　　　污水管 sewage pipe

drought [draʊt]

释义· *n.* 久旱；旱灾

例句· 干旱使供应给他们的水大为减少。

　　　　The drought has depleted their supply of water.

scrap [skræp]

释义· *adj.* 废弃的；报废的 *n.* 碎片；废品 *vt.* 废弃

例句· 这个湖里总有很多废塑料袋，湖水都是白色的。

　　　　There's always tons of scrap plastic bags in this lake, lake water in white.

搭配· 废金属 scrap metal

残羹剩饭 table/kitchen scraps

deplete [dɪˈpliːt]

释义· *vt.* 耗尽；使枯竭

例句· 耗尽世界的自然资源毋庸置疑是愚蠢的经济行为。

Surely it is an economic nonsense to deplete the world of natural resources.

派生· depletion *n.* 耗损；枯竭

landfill [ˈlændfɪl]

释义· *n.* 垃圾填埋场；垃圾堆填区

例句· 现代垃圾填埋场里的垃圾不会腐烂。

The rubbish in modern landfills does not rot.

搭配· 废物填埋场地 landfill site

viable [ˈvaɪəbl]

释义· *adj.* 能存活的；能生长发育的；切实可行的

例句· 只有少数林木可以从未授粉的胚珠发育成有活力的种子。

Only a few forest tree species can develop viable seed from unpollinated ovules.

派生· viability *n.* 可行性；生存能力

generation [ˌdʒenəˈreɪʃn]

释义· *n.* 一代人；一代

例句· 我们必须强调为子孙后代保护地球的必要性。

We must emphasize the need to preserve the planet for future generations.

搭配· 新一代；新生代 new generation

年轻的一代 / 老一辈 the younger/older generation

代代相传 from generation to generation

radiation [ˌreɪdi'eɪʃn]

释义· *n.* 辐射；放射物

例句· 他们遭受着健康问题的困扰并且害怕辐射的长期影响。

They suffer from health problems and fear the long term effects of radiation.

搭配· 辐射剂量 radiation dose

natural ['nætʃrəl]

释义· *adj.* 自然的；正常的；天生的 *n.* 有天赋的人

例句· 许多物种由于我们破坏了它们的自然栖息地而濒临灭绝。

Many species are in peril of extinction because of our destruction of their natural habitat.

搭配· 自然资源 natural resource

自然景观 natural landscape

回归自然 back to nature

本质上；事实上 in nature

理所当然地；自然地 in the nature of things

顺其自然；任其自然发展 let nature take its course

arid ['ærɪd]

释义· *adj.* 干旱的；干燥的；毫无新意的

例句· 尼罗河在埃及这一干旱地带形成了一个肥沃的漫滩，为原本贫瘠的地区提供了一条生命线。

The Nile River carves a fertile scar through this arid part of Egypt, providing a lifeline in an otherwise barren region.

派生· aridity *n.* 干旱；乏味

搭配· 干旱带 arid zone

catalyst ['kætəlɪst]

释义· *n.* 催化剂；刺激因素

例句· 我非常希望这起事件能催生变革。

I very much hope that this case will prove to be a catalyst for change.

搭配· 促使变化的人或引发变化的因素 a catalyst for sth.

pesticide ['pestɪsaɪd]

释义· *n.* 农药；杀虫剂；除害药物

例句· 例如，在印度的小麦种植区，农药和化肥的径流污染了高达 40% 的可用水源。

In India's wheat-growing regions, for example, pesticide and fertilizer runoff have polluted up to 40% of the available water supply.

搭配· 化学农药 chemical pesticide

农药残留（量）pesticide residue

滥用农药；滥用杀虫剂 pesticide abuse

erode [ɪ'roʊd]

释义· *v.* 侵蚀；腐蚀；损害；削弱

例句· 暴风雨冲走了建筑物和道路，侵蚀了沙滩。

The storm washed away buildings and roads and eroded beaches.

派生· erosion *n.* （气候等的）侵蚀，腐蚀；削弱

shameless ['ʃeɪmləs]

释义· *adj.* 无耻的；不知廉耻的；不要脸的

例句· 为了满足人们的欲望而杀死甚至毁灭动物是无耻的。

It is shameless to kill or even destroy animals to satisfy people's desires.

派生· shamelessness *n.* 无耻

fatal ['feɪtl]

释义· *adj.* 致命的；灾难性的

例句· 研究者发现，猪流感病毒比普通流感在肺更深部结合，这可以说明为什么它有时是致命的。

Researchers discover that the swine flu virus binds far deeper in the lungs than ordinary flu, possibly explaining why it is sometimes fatal.

派生· fatality *n.* 死亡；宿命

搭配· 绝症；不治之症　fatal disease

灾难性的错误　fatal error

致命的事故　fatal accident

destruction [dɪ'strʌkʃn]

释义· *n.* (U) 破坏；毁灭

例句· 洪水给该地区带来了死亡和破坏。

The floods brought death and destruction to the area.

同根· destructive *adj.* 破坏性的；毁灭性的

搭配· 栖息地破坏　habitat destruction

环境破坏　environmental destruction

ascribe [ə'skraɪb]

释义· *v.* 把……归因于；认为是……的特点

例句· 这份报告认为儿童哮喘发病率上升是因为污染加剧。

The report ascribes the rise in childhood asthma to the increase in pollution.

派生· ascription *n.* 归属；归因

搭配· 把某事归因于某人 / 某物 ascribe sth. to sb./sth.

disregard [ˌdɪsrɪˈɡɑːrd]

释义· *vt.* 无视；不顾；不理会 *n.* (U) 忽视

例句· 董事会完全无视我的建议。

The board completely disregarded my recommendations.

搭配· 忽视某人 / 某物 disregard for/of sb./sth.

modernization [ˌmɑːdərnəˈzeɪʃn]

释义· *n.* (U) 现代化

例句· 我们必须实现科学技术现代化，否则我们要落后于其他国家。

We must achieve modernization of science and technology, otherwise we will lag behind other nations.

同根· modernistic *adj.* （建筑、家具等）现代化的，摩登的

organic [ɔːrˈɡænɪk]

释义· *adj.* 有机的；绿色的；生物的

例句· 施粪肥之类的有机物能够改良土壤。

Adding organic matter such as manure can improve the soil.

搭配· 有机农业 organic agriculture

有机食品 organic food

有机物 organic substance/matter

detriment [ˈdetrɪmənt]

释义· *n.* 损害；伤害

例句· 许多国家像日本一样过度捕捞，损害海洋环境。

Many countries overfished, just like Japan, to the detriment of the ocean environment.

派生· detrimental *adj.* 有害的；不利的

搭配· 对某人 / 某事不利

　　　to the detriment of sb./sth. & to sb.'s/sth.'s detriment

species ['spiːʃiːz]

释义· *n.* 物种；种类

例句· 大多数本地哺乳动物的数量都已经大大减少了。

　　　Most native mammal species have been severely depleted.

搭配· 物种多样性　species diversity

　　　物种丰富度　species richness

valid ['vælɪd]

释义· *adj.* 合法的；有效的；正当的

例句· 在规定的时间狩猎是合法的，但不能捕杀受保护的动物。

　　　It is valid to hunt in the stipulated time, but not to kill

　　　protected animals.

反义· invalid *adj.* 无效的 *n.* 病弱者 *vt.* 令……退役

派生· validity *n.*（法律上的）有效，合法性

搭配· 有效期　valid date

　　　有效期限　valid period

traumatic [trɑʊ'mætɪk]

释义· *adj.* 创伤的；痛苦的

例句· 对孩子来说，一只宠物的死亡可能会造成心理创伤。

　　　For a child the death of a pet can be traumatic.

搭配· 惨痛的经历　traumatic experience

brutal ['bruːtl]

释义· *adj.* 野蛮的；残暴的；直截了当的

例句· 人类对动物犯下了多少野蛮的行径？

　　　How many brutal acts have humans committed against

animals?

派生· brutality *n.* 野蛮行径；残暴行为

pristine ['prɪstiːn]

释义· *adj.* 原始的；未开发的；崭新的

例句· 犹他州有着一些美国的最原始和最美丽的国家公园。

Utah has some of the most pristine and beautiful national parks in the United States.

搭配· 净土 pristine land

solar ['soʊlər]

释义· *adj.* 太阳的；太阳能的

例句· 我们对太阳活动知道得越多，就越能更好地保护我们自己。

The more we know about solar activity, the better we can protect ourselves.

搭配· 太阳能 solar energy/power

太阳辐射 solar radiation

太阳能电池 solar cell

vaccine [væk'siːn]

释义· *n.* 疫苗

例句· 科学家正在研究疫苗生产的新方法，但是在这场大流行病发生前疫苗无法及时准备好。

Scientists are working on new methods of vaccine production but nothing will be ready in time for this pandemic.

doom [duːm]

释义· *vt.* 使……注定失败（或遭殃、死亡等）*n.* (U) 死亡；厄运

例句· 许多物种注定要灭绝。

Many species are doomed to extinction.

派生· doomed *adj.* 注定的

搭配· 注定要做某事 be doomed to do sth.

悲观失望；无望 doom and gloom/gloom and doom

overnight [ˌoʊvərˈnaɪt]

释义· *adv.* 一夜之间；突然；在夜间

例句· 沙漠不会一夜之间变成森林，植树造林是一个漫长的过程。

Deserts are not changed to forests overnight, and the afforestation is a long process.

搭配· 一夜成名 overnight fame

暴发户 overnight millionaire

intolerable [ɪnˈtɑːlərəbl]

释义· *adj.* 无法忍受的；不能容忍的

例句· 他们觉得这会给他们带来无法承受的压力。

They felt this would put intolerable pressure on them.

搭配· 无法承受的负担 intolerable burden

baneful [ˈbeɪnfl]

释义· *adj.* 有害的；有毒的

例句· 为了减少有害排放和节约能源，许多国家正在积极开发新能源技术和寻找替代燃料。

To reduce baneful emission and save energy, many countries are actively developing new energy technology and searching for alternative fuel.

搭配· 恶劣影响 baneful influence

fertilizer [ˈfɜːrtəlaɪzər]

释义· *n.* 肥料

例句· 除了减少运输过程中的碳排放，有机食品通常使用动物粪便作为肥料。

In addition to the carbon savings in transportation, such foods rely on animal manure as fertilizer.

搭配· 有机肥 organic fertilizer

化学肥料 chemical fertilizers

degrade [dɪˈɡreɪd]

释义· *v.* 使恶化；使退化；降低……身份

例句· 海豚的栖息环境正遭到越发严重的破坏。

The dolphin's habitat is being rapidly degraded.

派生· degradable *adj.* 可降解的

degradation *n.* 退化；堕落

搭配· （通过做某事）自贬身份 degrade yourself (by doing sth.)

降低性能 degrade performance

levy [ˈlevi]

释义· *v.* 征收；征（税）*n.* 税款

例句· 政府应该向那些造成严重污染的企业征收更高的税。

The government should levy higher taxes on companies that cause severe pollution.

搭配· （对某物）征税 / 收费 / 罚款 levy a tax/charge/fine (on sth.)

surveillance [sɜːrˈveɪləns]

释义· *n.* (U) 监视；监察

例句· 该公司计划在隧道两端安装监视设备。

The company is planning to place surveillance equipment at both ends of the tunnel.

搭配· 受到监视 under surveillance

电子监控设备　electronic surveillance equipment

监控摄像机　surveillance camera

mercy ['mɜːrsi]

释义· *n.* 仁慈；宽容

例句· 双方都没有抓俘虏，也没有表现出丝毫的心慈手软。

Neither side took prisoners or showed any mercy.

派生· merciful *adj.* 仁慈的；慈悲的

搭配· 任由某人 / 某物摆布　at the mercy of sb./sth.

指望某人能够善待（或宽恕）你　throw yourself on sb.'s mercy

幸运的是……　it's a mercy (that)

残忍地；毫不留情地　without mercy

安乐死　mercy killing

cataclysm ['kætəklɪzəm]

释义· *n.* 大灾难；剧变

例句· 这些大灭绝中最近的一次也是人们最熟悉的一次，终结了恐龙时代。

The most recent of the Big Five is the most familiar one—the cataclysm that ended the Age of Dinosaurs.

派生· cataclysmic *adj.* 灾难性的；引起巨大变化的

poach [poʊtʃ]

释义· *v.* （在他人地界）偷猎，偷捕；盗用；挖走（人员等）

例句· 很多旨在为野生动物提供庇护的国家公园经常受到偷猎者的入侵。

Many national parks set up to provide a refuge for wildlife are regularly invaded by people poaching game.

派生· poaching *n.* 偷猎

poacher *n.* 偷猎者

搭配· 侵犯某人的职权 poach on one's territory

ecology [i'kɑ:lədʒi]

释义· *n.* (U) 生态；生态学

例句· 石油污染可能破坏珊瑚礁脆弱的生态环境。

Oil pollution could damage the fragile ecology of the coral reefs.

派生· ecological *adj.* 生态的；生态学的

搭配· 植物 / 动物 / 人类生态学 plant/animal/human ecology

wildlife ['waɪldlaɪf]

释义· *n.* (U) 野生生物；野生动物

例句· 开发这一地区将会危及野生生物。

Development of the area would endanger wildlife.

搭配· 野生动物园 wildlife park

野生动物保护区 wildlife refuge

野生生物保护 wildlife conservation

haze [heɪz]

释义· *n.* 雾霭；（阴）霾；迷糊 *v.* （使）笼罩在薄雾中

例句· 当你凝视中国的雾霾，你就会感到绝望。

When you peer into the haze in China, you will be in despair.

搭配· 特指中国由烧煤引起的雾霾 coal toxic haze

discharge [dɪs'tʃɑ:rdʒ]

释义· *v.* 排出；放出；解雇 *n.* 排出（物）

例句· 污水直接排入海里。

Sewage is discharged directly into the sea.

搭配· 准许某人离开…… discharge sb. from sth.

把 A 排入 B discharge sth. into sth.

排污 pollution discharge

overuse [ˌoʊvərˈjuːs]

释义· *n.* (U) 滥用

例句· 由于滥用和污染，淡水供应正受到日益严重的威胁。

Water supplies are under increasing threat from overuse and pollution.

fossil [ˈfɑːsl]

释义· *n.* 化石；思想僵化的人

例句· 化石燃料（如煤和石油）属于有限资源。

The fossil fuels (coal and oil) are finite resources.

派生· fossilize *v.* （使）变成化石，石化；（使人或物）僵化

搭配· 化石燃料；矿物燃料 fossil fuel

释义	短语
对……构成威胁	pose a threat to
化学反应	chemical reaction
把 A 归咎于 B	blame A on B
环保的	eco-friendly/environmental sound
有害污染物	noxious pollutants
酸雨	acid rain
紫外线	ultraviolet ray
颗粒物质	particulate matter (PM)
温室气体	heat-trapping gases/greenhouse gases
温室效应	green-house effect
全球变暖	global warming
免疫系统	immune system
脆弱的生态平衡	delicate ecological balance
增加农产品产量	boost crop yield
齐心协力做某事	make a concerted effort to do sth.
过度依赖	be unduly reliant/depend on
臭氧层	ozone layer
失去植被	loss of vegetation

对……施加压力	put a strain on sth.
对……造成伤害	wreak damage to
超过法定标准	exceed legally established limits
呼吸道疾病	respiratory disease
融合最新科技	incorporate the latest technology
人类活动	anthropogenic activities/human-related activities
扭转环境恶化	reverse environmental deterioration
以……为代价	at the expense of
提高公众某方面的意识	raise the public awareness of sth.
耕地	arable land
对……有不利影响	have an adverse effect on
处于次要地位；退居二线	take a back seat
拯救许多动物免遭灭绝	save many animals from extinction
预防为主，治疗为辅。（一分的预防，胜过十分的治疗。）	An ounce of prevention is worth a pound of cure.

巩 固 练 习

练习1 根据下面的中文释义，写出对应的单词（词组）。

A	B
使恶化 d_____	野生生物 w_____
化石 f_____	污染 c_____
合法的 v_____	吸入 i_____
保护 c_____	有毒的 t_____
肮脏的 f_____	生态系统 e_____
调整 a_____	慢性的 c_____
污染物 p_____	耕地 a_____
野蛮的 b_____	人为活动 a_____
呼吸道疾病 r_____	偷猎 p_____
全球变暖 g_____	腐烂 d_____
温室气体 h_____	恢复 r_____

练习2 用方框中所给单词（词组）的适当形式填空。

adapt	shortage	catalyst	mercy	cruel
exceed	lessen	contribute to	discharge	deplete
detriment	disregard	alter	intolerable	disgrace

1. How do these insects a_____ (适应) themselves to new environments?

2. Now the pollution rate has e_____ (超过) the carrying capacity

of the environment.

3. It would be a d＿＿＿＿（耻辱）for human beings to harm, and even destroy other species for their own sake.

4. The water s＿＿＿＿（缺乏）in this country is potentially catastrophic.

5. I can't stand people who are c＿＿＿＿（残忍的）to animals.

6. I believe that each of us can c＿＿＿＿（有助于）the improvement of the world environment.

7. The landscape has been radically a＿＿＿＿（改变）, severely damaging wildlife.

8. The new project will l＿＿＿＿（减轻）the effects of car pollution.

9. Surely it is an economic nonsense to d＿＿＿＿（耗尽）the world of natural resources.

10. I very much hope that this case will prove to be a c＿＿＿＿（催化剂）for change.

11. The board completely d＿＿＿＿（无视）my recommendations.

12. Many countries overfished, just like Japan, to the d＿＿＿＿（损害）of the ocean environment.

13. They felt this would put i＿＿＿＿（无法忍受的）pressure on them.

14. Neither side took prisoners or showed any m＿＿＿＿（仁慈）.

15. Sewage is d＿＿＿＿（排出）directly into the sea.

☐ pollutant	☐ ecosystem	☐ emission
☐ recycle	☐ crude	☐ unwarranted
☐ primitive	☐ shortage	☐ fumes
☐ adapt	☐ scarcity	☐ outweigh
☐ hostile	☐ disastrous	☐ mirror
☐ groundless	☐ toxic	☐ evolution
☐ minimize	☐ poisonous	☐ alter
☐ foul	☐ barbaric	☐ equilibrium
☐ conserve	☐ cruel	☐ infertile
☐ decline	☐ origin	☐ dissipate
☐ adjustment	☐ filter	☐ smog
☐ exceed	☐ supply	☐ decompose
☐ convert	☐ distaste	☐ gradually
☐ mine	☐ purify	☐ lessen
☐ restore	☐ contribute	☐ sensitive
☐ posterity	☐ torture	☐ cripple
☐ chronic	☐ ruin	☐ penetrate
☐ inhabit	☐ subject	☐ severe
☐ pointlessly	☐ inhale	☐ questionable
☐ endanger	☐ deforestation	☐ sewage
☐ disgrace	☐ irreversible	☐ drought
☐ culprit	☐ dearth	☐ scrap
☐ irrigation	☐ contaminate	☐ deplete
☐ remedial	☐ reclaim	☐ landfill

☐ viable	☐ organic	☐ degrade
☐ generation	☐ detriment	☐ levy
☐ radiation	☐ species	☐ surveillance
☐ natural	☐ valid	☐ mercy
☐ arid	☐ traumatic	☐ cataclysm
☐ catalyst	☐ brutal	☐ poach
☐ pesticide	☐ pristine	☐ ecology
☐ erode	☐ solar	☐ wildlife
☐ shameless	☐ vaccine	☐ haze
☐ fatal	☐ doom	☐ discharge
☐ destruction	☐ overnight	☐ overuse
☐ ascribe	☐ intolerable	☐ fossil
☐ disregard	☐ baneful	
☐ modernization	☐ fertilizer	

表中共有 112 个单词

您不确认的单词 _____ 个，占总数的 _____%

如果比例高于 10%，请耐心再复习一遍。如果比例低于 10%，您可以开始下一章的托福写作之旅了！

第六章

政治社会

abolish [əˈbɑːlɪʃ]

释义· *vt.* 废除，废止（法律、制度、习俗等）

例句· 这些改革措施将彻底废除带有种族歧视的法律。

These reforms will abolish racially discriminatory laws.

派生· abolishable *adj.* 可废止的；可废除的

legalize [ˈliːgəlaɪz]

释义· *vt.* 使合法化

例句· 最近，英国属地曼岛政府做出一个备受争议的决定——使安乐死合法化。

Recently, the government on the Isle of Man has made a much debated decision to legalize euthanasia.

同根· legality *n.* 合法（性）

boom [buːm]

释义· *n.* （经济的）繁荣 *v.* 繁荣；激增

例句·　经济很快就从繁荣走向了萧条。

　　　The economy went from boom to bust very quickly.

派生·　booming *adj.* 兴旺的；繁荣的

搭配·　经济繁荣　economic boom

　　　景气年；经济高度增长年　boom year

　　　繁荣与萧条　boom and bust

deteriorate [dɪ'tɪrɪəreɪt]

释义·　*v.* 恶化；变坏

例句·　美国经济持续恶化，不断攀升的失业率即为明证。

　　　The US economy continues to deteriorate as reflected in surging unemployment.

派生·　deterioration *n.* 恶化；退化

crisis ['kraɪsɪs]

释义·　*n.* 危机；紧要关头

例句·　政府宣布市场不景气是由亚洲金融危机引起的。

　　　The government predicates that the market collapse was caused by the Asian financial crisis.

搭配·　信任危机　crisis of confidence

　　　金融危机　financial crisis

　　　经济危机　economic crisis

扩展·　crises (*pl.*)

broadcast ['brɔːdkæst]

释义·　*n.* 广播；广播节目 *v.* 广播；传播

例句·　在许多地方，政府对印刷媒体与对广播媒体的内容有不同的控制权。

　　　In many jurisdictions, the government's power to regulate

content differs between print and broadcast media.

派生· broadcaster *n.* 广播员；电视台

搭配· 新闻广播 news broadcast

扩展· broadcast（过去式）broadcast（过去分词）

reinforce [ˌriːɪnˈfɔːrs]

释义· *v.* 加强；加固；增援

例句· 他们担心一个更加强大的欧洲议会只会增强大国的力量。

A stronger European Parliament would, they fear, only reinforce the power of the larger countries.

派生· reinforcement *n.* 巩固；加强

reinforced *adj.* 加固的；加强的

disrupt [dɪsˈrʌpt]

释义· *vt.* 扰乱；使中断；打乱

例句· 那些在我们国家或任何其他国家破坏信息自由流通的人对我们的经济、政府和公民社会构成了威胁。

Those who disrupt the free flow of information in our society or any other pose a threat to our economy, our government, and our civil society.

派生· disruption *n.* 中断；扰乱

disruptive *adj.* 破坏性的；引起混乱的

establish [ɪˈstæblɪʃ]

释义· *v.* 建立；设立；确立

例句· 政府的目标是在北方建立一个新的研究中心。

The government's goal is to establish a new research center in the North.

派生· established *adj.* 确定的；著名的

establishment *n.* 确立；建立

搭配· 确立某人自己在……的地位 establish oneself in sth.

确立为……；使成为…… establish as

创业 establish a business

circumstance ['sɜːrkəmstæns]

释义· *n.* 形势；情况；环境

例句· 政府颁布了许多法律来改变目前的经济形势。

The government has enacted many laws to change the current economic circumstance.

搭配· 绝不；无论如何不 in/under no circumstances

在这种情况下；既然如此 in/under the circumstances

plague [pleɪg]

释义· *vt.* 困扰；折磨 *n.* 瘟疫；麻烦

例句· 交通拥堵问题一直困扰着这个城市的政府部门。

Traffic jams have been plaguing this city's government.

搭配· 受到某事的困扰 be plagued by sth.

某人饱受某事的困扰 plague sb. with sth.

prohibit [prə'hɪbɪt]

释义· *vt.* 禁止；阻止

例句· 几乎所有国家都禁止在公共场所吸烟。

In almost all countries, smoking in public is prohibited.

派生· prohibition *n.* 禁止；禁令

prohibitive *adj.* （价格）高得令人负担不起的；禁止的

搭配· 禁止某人做某事 prohibit sb. from doing sth.

dispose [dɪ'spoʊz]

释义· *v.* 处理；处置；安排

例句· 市政府每天都会处理掉成千上万吨的生活垃圾。

The city government disposed of tens of thousands of tons of household waste every day.

派生· disposed *adj.* 倾向于；有意于

disposal *n.* 去掉；处理

搭配· 使某人倾向于某种感觉或想法　dispose sb. to/towards sth.

击败某人 / 处理某物　dispose of sb./sth.

coexist [ˌkoʊɪgˈzɪst]

释义· *vi.* 共存；（尤指）和平共处

例句· 政府采取了开放的政策，因此不同的文化曾和平共存了很多年。

The government adopted an open policy, so the different cultures had coexisted peacefully for many years.

派生· coexistence *n.* 共存

enact [ɪˈnækt]

释义· *vt.* 颁布；制定法律；扮演

例句· 政府官员也说他们计划在 2011 年末颁布国家第一部慈善法。

Government officials have also said that they plan to enact the nation's first charity law by late 2011.

派生· enactment *n.*（法律的）制定，通过

penalty [ˈpenəlti]

释义· *n.* 刑罚；处罚；惩罚；报应

例句· 国际特赦组织反对死刑，称其违背了生命权。

Amnesty International opposes the death penalty as a violation of the right to life.

同根· penalize *vt.* 处罚

搭配· 某事的弊端　penalty of sth.

对某事的处罚　penalty for sth.

死刑　death penalty

bureaucracy [bjʊˈrɑːkrəsi]

释义· *n.* 官僚主义；官僚制度

例句· 我们政府面临的最大的问题就是官僚主义。

The biggest problem our government faces is the bureaucracy.

同根· bureaucratic *adj.* 官僚主义的

tackle [ˈtækl]

释义· *v.* 解决；处理；对付；与……交涉

例句· 政府决心解决通货膨胀问题。

The government is determined to tackle inflation.

搭配· 就某事与某人交涉　tackle sb. about sth.

incident [ˈɪnsɪdənt]

释义· *n.* 事件；事故

例句· 这些事件是两国之间一系列争端中最新的几起。

These incidents were the latest in a series of disputes between the two nations.

派生· incidental *adj.* 附带的；伴随的

incidence *n.* （多指坏事）发生率

prerequisite [ˌpriːˈrekwəzɪt]

释义· *n.* 先决条件；前提

例句· 成为党员是事业有成必不可少的先决条件。

Party membership was an essential prerequisite of a successful career.

搭配· 预修课程　prerequisite course

dominate ['dɑːmɪneɪt]

释义· *v.* 控制；支配；占优势地位

例句· 一些非常重要的领域由政府主导，比如军事和能源行业。

Some very important areas are dominated by the government, such as the industry of military and energy.

派生· domination *n.* 控制；支配

搭配· 支配；统治 dominate over

congress ['kɑːŋgrəs]

释义· *n.* 国会；议会；代表大会

例句· 这项法律应对每个国会议员和公民都有意义。

This law should mean something to every member of Congress and every citizen.

派生· congressman *n.* 国会议员

congressional *adj.* 立法机构的；国会的

guidance ['gaɪdns]

释义· *n.* (U) 引导；指导；导航

例句· 经济发展往往需要政府的引导。

Economic development often requires government guidance.

同根· guideline *n.* 指导方针

搭配· 在……的指导下 under the guidance of

就业指导 career guidance

emerge [i'mɜːrdʒ]

释义· *vi.* 出现；浮现；显露

例句· 但是除此之外，将出现一种经济现象，那就是，中国制造不只向国外销售，也会在国内购买。

But out of it will emerge an economy where Made in China is not just sold abroad, but bought at home too.

派生· emergence *n.* 出现；兴起

搭配· 自……出现；从……显露出来 emerge from

forbid [fər'bɪd]

释义· *vt.* 禁止；不允许

例句· 有的国家禁止难民送自己的孩子进当地学校念书。
Some countries forbid refugees from sending their children to local schools.

派生· forbidden *adj.* 禁止的；不准的

搭配· 禁止某人做某事 forbid sb. to do sth./forbid sb. from doing sth.

扩展· forbade（过去式）forbidden（过去分词）

majority [mə'dʒɔːrəti]

释义· *n.*（获胜的）票数；多数票；大部分；大多数

例句· 工党在上次大选中赢得了绝大多数选票。
The Labor Party won a huge majority at the last general election.

反义· minority *n.* 少数；少数派；少数民族

搭配· 占多数 in a/the majority

collapse [kə'læps]

释义· *n.* 崩溃；暴跌；突然失败；倒塌 *v.* 崩溃；瓦解；倒塌

例句· 人们也认为这一制度的崩溃带来了各种新的可能性。
It was also felt that the collapse of the system opened up new possibilities.

legislation [ˌledʒɪs'leɪʃn]

释义· *n.* (U) 法律；立法

例句· 政府承诺颁行新法规来解决这个问题。

The government has promised to bring in new legislation to combat this problem.

同根· legislative *adj.* 立法的；制定法律的

conservative [kən'sɜːrvətɪv]

释义· *adj.* 保守的；守旧的 *n.* 保守者

例句· 公民们在任何选举中都千篇一律地支持最保守的候选人。

Citizens invariably support the most conservative candidate in any election.

同根· conservation *n.* 保护；保持

conservatism *n.* 守旧；保守主义

搭配· 保守党 conservative party

substantiate [səb'stænʃieɪt]

释义· *vt.* 证明；证实

例句· 然而，政府当时的解释并没有证实这些谣言。

However, contemporary accounts from the government did not substantiate these rumors.

派生· substantiation *n.* 证明；证实

exaggerate [ɪɡ'zædʒəreɪt]

释义· *v.* 夸大；夸张

例句· 政府经常夸大一些数据或事实以获得广泛的支持。

Governments often exaggerate some data or facts to gain widespread support.

派生· exaggerated *adj.* 夸大的；夸张的

exaggeration *n.* 夸大；夸张

urge [ɜːrdʒ]

释义· *v.* 敦促；竭力主张；驱赶 *n.* 强烈的欲望；冲动

例句· 他们敦促国会批准他们有关改革项目的计划。

They urged Congress to approve plans for their reform programme.

派生· urgency *n.* 紧急；紧急的事

搭配· 向某人大力推荐某事 urge sth. on/upon sb.

敦促某人做某事 urge sb. to do sth.

delinquency [dɪ'lɪŋkwənsi]

释义· *n.*（尤指青少年的）违法行为，犯罪行为

例句· 青少年犯罪是这个国家一个严重的社会问题。

Juvenile delinquency is a serious social problem in this country.

搭配· 青少年犯罪 juvenile delinquency

publicity [pʌb'lɪsəti]

释义· *n.* (U) 宣传；（媒体或公众的）关注

例句· 政府鼓励他们将森林问题纳入其宣传或慈善工作。

The government encouraged them to integrate forests into their publicity or philanthropic work.

同根· publicize *vt.* 宣传；宣扬；推广

搭配· 作秀；炒作 publicity stunt

inevitable [ɪn'evɪtəbl]

释义· *adj.* 不可避免的；必然发生的

例句· 战败对英国政策不可避免地产生了影响。

The defeat had inevitable consequences for British policy.

派生· inevitability *n.* 不可避免；无法规避

combat ['kɑːmbæt]

释义· *v.* 打击；防止；减轻；战斗 *n.* 战斗

例句· 国会对政府打击犯罪的新措施提出了批评。

Congress has criticised new government measures to combat crime.

派生· combative *adj.* 好战的；好斗的

搭配· 为……奋斗 combat for

estate [ɪ'steɪt]

释义· *n.* 地产；个人财产；（尤指）遗产；庄园

例句· 中国政府通过宏观政策来管控流向房地产的资金。

The Chinese government controls the flow of money into real estate through macro-policies.

搭配· 不动产；房地产 real estate

metropolis [mə'trɑːpəlɪs]

释义· *n.* 大都会；首都

例句· 伦敦是一个多元文化的大都市，充满活力和个性。

London is a multicultural metropolis with a vibrancy and a personality all its own.

survey ['sɜːrveɪ]

释义· *n.* 调查；测量

例句· 市政会就农场建筑的使用情况进行了调查。

The council conducted a survey of the uses to which farm buildings are put.

搭配· 实地调查；实地考察 field survey

foundation [faʊnˈdeɪʃn]

释义· *n.* 根基；基础；基金会
例句· 这个问题严重影响了我们社会的基本根基。
The issue strikes at the very foundation of our community.
派生· foundational *adj.* 基础的；基本的

undergo [ˌʌndərˈɡoʊ]

释义· *vt.* 经历；经受；遭受
例句· 这个国家最近经历了巨大的变化。
The country has undergone massive changes recently.
扩展· underwent（过去式）undergone（过去分词）

beneficiary [ˌbenɪˈfɪʃieri]

释义· *n.* 受益者；受惠人
例句· 迄今为止，退休金均等政策的主要受益者一直是男性。
The main beneficiaries of pension equality so far have been men.

revenue [ˈrevənuː]

释义· *n.* 税收收入；收益
例句· 非常有钱的人每人支付的税也最多，但是大部分的税收却来自那些不那么富有的人。
The very wealthy pay the most taxes per person, but the bulk of tax revenue comes from those who are not so wealthy.
搭配· 税收 tax revenue
总收入 total revenue
收支 revenue and expenditure

proportion [prə'pɔːrʃn]

释义· *n.* 比例；部分；均衡

例句· 从事该职业的女性比例已升高到 17.3%。

The proportion of women in the profession had risen to 17.3%.

搭配· 成比例；相称 in proportion

与某物不相称 out of (all) proportion to sth.

一大部分…… a large proportion of

正比 direct proportion

aggravate ['æɡrəveɪt]

释义· *vt.* 使严重；使恶化；激怒

例句· 由于利率上调，他们的资金问题更加严重。

Their money problems were further aggravated by a rise in interest rates.

派生· aggravated *adj.* 加重的；严重的

aggravation *n.* 加剧；激怒

fiscal ['fɪskl]

释义· *adj.* 财政的

例句· 所有的经济问题都与这个国家面临的长期财政挑战这一核心问题有关。

All the economic issues are tied, to the same core problem which is the long-term fiscal challenge that this country faces.

搭配· 一个财政问题 a fiscal matter

财政赤字 fiscal deficit

财政预算 fiscal budget

commit [kə'mɪt]

释义· *v.* 承诺，保证（做）；犯（错误或罪行）

例句· 他明确地作出保证，他的政府会继续在经济改革的道路上走下去。

He has clearly committed his government to continuing down the path of economic reform.

派生· committed *adj.* 坚定的；尽心尽力的

搭配· 向某人承诺做某事 commit sb. to doing sth.

把某事学好记牢 commit sth. to memory

犯罪；犯下罪行 commit a crime

自杀 commit suicide

扩展· committed（过去式）committed（过去分词）

influential [ˌɪnflu'enʃl]

释义· *adj.* 有影响力的；有权势的

例句· 这位市长在制定经济政策方面曾起过很大作用。

This mayor had been influential in shaping economic policy.

搭配· 重要作用；重要角色 influential role

subsidy ['sʌbsədi]

释义· *n.* 补贴；津贴；补助金

例句· 在许多国家，油价被人为压低，要么通过法令，要么通过补贴。

In many countries, oil prices are held artificially low, either by fiat or subsidy.

派生· subsidize *vt.* 资助；给……发津贴

democracy [dɪ'mɑːkrəsi]

释义· *n.* 民主；民主政治；民主制度

例句· 他假意支持多党民主和人权问题。

He was making all the right noises about multi-party

democracy and human rights.

同根· democratic *adj.* 民主的；民主管理的

virtue ['vɜːrtʃuː]

释义· *n.* 美德；优点

例句· 政府正在大力向公民宣传各种传统美德。

The government is vigorously promoting all kinds of traditional virtues for the citizen.

搭配· 凭借某物 by/in virtue of

善与恶 virtue and vice

公民道德 civic virtue

美德的典范 a paragon of virtue

corrupt [kəˈrʌpt]

释义· *adj.* 腐败的；贪污的；受贿的 *v.* 使堕落；破坏

例句· 腐败的政府官员向他敲诈钱财。

Corrupt government officials were extorting money from him.

派生· corruption *n.* 贪污；受贿；使人堕落的行为

搭配· 徇私舞弊 corrupt practices

interfere [ˌɪntərˈfɪr]

释义· *v.* 干涉；妨碍；介入

例句· 联合国不能干涉任何国家的内政。

The UN cannot interfere in the internal affairs of any country.

派生· interference *n.* 干涉；干预；介入

搭配· 干扰某人 interfere with sb.

干涉某事 interfere in sth.

intrusion [ɪn'truːʒn]

释义· *n.* 侵入；干扰

例句· 禁止非法搜查或者非法侵入公民的住宅。

Unlawful search of, or intrusion into, a citizen's home is prohibited.

同根· intrusive *adj.* 侵入的；闯入的

municipal [mjuː'nɪsɪpl]

释义· *adj.* 市政的；城市的

例句· 市政当局批准了这次游行。

The municipal authorities gave the go-ahead for the march.

派生· municipality *n.* 自治市

搭配· 市政府　municipal government

stringent ['strɪndʒənt]

释义· *adj.*（尤指法律、规章、标准等）严格的；（经济）紧缩的

例句· 他宣布将对武器的持有实行更严格的控制。

He announced that there would be more stringent controls on the possession of weapons.

派生· stringency *n.* 财政紧缩；手头紧

citizen ['sɪtɪzn]

释义· *n.* 公民；市民

例句· 每个公民都可以要求受到法律的保护。

Every citizen may claim the protection of the law.

派生· citizenship *n.* 公民权利；公民身份

搭配· 网民　net citizen

hierarchy ['haɪərɑːrki]

释义· *n.* 等级制度；统治集团

例句· 等级制度在原则上并不等同于极权主义恐怖。

The principle of hierarchy does not equate to totalitarian terror.

派生· hierarchical *adj.* 按等级划分的；等级制度的

搭配· 社会 / 政治等级制度 the social/political hierarchy

知识体系 knowledge hierarchy

exclude [ɪk'skluːd]

释义· *vt.* 阻止……参加；不放在考虑之列；不包括

例句· 伦敦有些俱乐部仍然拒绝妇女参加。

Women are still excluded from some London clubs.

派生· exclusive *adj.* 独有的；排外的；高级的

搭配· 阻止某人参加某事 exclude sb. from sth.

distribution [ˌdɪstrɪ'bjuːʃn]

释义· *n.* 分配；分发；分布

例句· 社会主义社会的分配原则是"各尽所能"，"按劳分配"。

The principle of distribution in socialist society is "from each according to his ability" and "to each according to his work".

搭配· 财富分配不公 the unfair distribution of wealth

devastate ['devəsteɪt]

释义· *vt.* 摧毁；毁灭；彻底破坏；使震惊

例句· 中国可以提高利率来抑制高物价，但是这会摧毁增长。

China could increase interest rates to temper rising prices, but that would devastate growth.

派生· devastating *adj.* 毁灭性的；令人震惊的

ban [bæn]

释义· *n.* 禁令 *vt.* 禁止；取缔

例句· 政府实施了彻底的猎狐禁令。

The government has imposed an outright ban on fox hunting.

搭配· 禁止某人做某事 ban sb. from doing sth.

扩展· banned（过去式）banned（过去分词）

ideology [ˌaɪdi'ɑːlədʒi]

释义· *n.* 意识形态；思想意识

例句· 这种方法与社会主义意识形态的原则相符。

Such an approach accords with the principles of socialist ideology.

派生· ideological *adj.* 思想体系的；意识形态的

principle ['prɪnsəpl]

释义· *n.* 原则；原理

例句· 国家的独立和主权平等是国际法上的一项根本原则。

Independence and sovereign equality among states is a fundamental principle of international law.

搭配· 理论上；原则上；大体上 in principle

根据……的原则 on the principle of

conceal [kən'siːl]

释义· *vt.* 隐瞒；隐藏

例句· 政府隐瞒的真相迟早会被揭露。

Sooner or later, the truth that the government concealed will be revealed.

搭配· 向某人隐藏某物 conceal sth. from sb.

scrutiny ['skru:təni]

释义· *n.* (U) 仔细检查；认真彻底的审查

例句· 总统承诺政府将接受公众监督。

The President promised a government open to public scrutiny.

派生· scrutinize *v.* 仔细检查；认真查看

individual [ˌɪndɪ'vɪdʒuəl]

释义· *n.* 个人；个体 *adj.* 个人的；单独的；个别的；独特的

例句· 任何人不得凌驾于法律之上。

No individual shall overtop the law.

派生· individualism *n.* 个人主义；个性

allocate ['æləkeɪt]

释义· *v.* 分配；分派；划拨

例句· 1985 年联邦预算将 73 亿美元拨给了开发项目。

The 1985 federal budget allocated $7.3 billion for development programmes.

搭配· 把……拨给 allocate for

把某物分配给某人 / 某事 allocate sth. to sb./sth.

declare [dɪ'kler]

释义· *v.* 声明；宣布；断言

例句· 他声明不再竞选连任总统。

He declared he would not run for a second term as president.

搭配· 声明反对某人 / 某事 declare against sb./sth.

声明支持某人 / 某事 declare for sb./sth.

发表意见；显露身份 declare oneself

investment [ɪn'vestmənt]

释义· *n.* 投资；（时间、精力的）投入

例句· 政府急于吸引外资来资助建设项目。

The government is eager to attract foreign investment to fund building projects.

搭配· 对某物进行投资 investment in sth.

entitle [ɪn'taɪtl]

释义· *vt.* 给予……权利；给予……资格；给……命名

例句· 目前的法律法规赋予教师太多的责任和义务，但权利却很少。

Current laws and regulations entitle many obligations and responsibilities to teachers, but too few rights.

派生· entitled *adj.* 有资格的 entitlement *n.* 权利

搭配· 使某人享有某物 entitle sb. to sth.

给予某人做某事的权利 entitle sb. to do sth.

flourish ['flɜːrɪʃ]

释义· *vi.* 繁荣；兴旺 *vt.* 挥舞 *n.* 夸张动作

例句· 在目前的经济环境下，很少有企业兴旺发达。

Few businesses are flourishing in the present economic climate.

派生· flourishing *adj.* 繁荣的；盛行的

搭配· 在全盛期；盛极一时 in full flourish

用引人注意的动作；用夸张的动作 with a flourish

security [sə'kjʊrəti]

释义· *n.* 保护措施；安全工作；安全感

例句· 首都采取了严密的安全措施。

Strict security measures are in force in the capital.

搭配· 社会保险；社会保障 social security

公共安全 public security

安检 security check

budget ['bʌdʒɪt]

释义· *n.* 预算 *v.* 把……编入预算 *adj.* 低价的

例句· 我们必须削减国防预算。

We had to make cuts in the defense budget.

搭配· 钱不多的；控制预算的 on a budget

财政预算 financial budget

expand [ɪk'spænd]

释义· *v.* 详细阐明；扩大；增加

例句· 总统利用今天的演讲更充分地阐述了他上个月所讲的话。

The president used today's speech to expand on remarks he made last month.

派生· expansion *n.* 扩大；增加；膨胀

搭配· 详述某事 expand on/upon sth.

扩大为某物 expand into sth.

confine [kən'faɪn]

释义· *vt.* 限制，限定（防止扩散蔓延）；监禁；关押

例句· 卫生官员们已经成功地把疫情控制在塔巴廷加地区。

Health officials have successfully confined the epidemic to the Tabatinga area.

派生· confined *adj.* 狭小的；有限的

confinement *n.* 禁闭；监禁；分娩

搭配· 把某人／某物限制在…… confine sb./sth. to sth.

被局限在…… be confined in sth.

demolish [dɪ'mɑːlɪʃ]

释义· *vt.* 拆毁；毁掉；驳倒（观点或理论）

例句· 专家建议政府拆除市中心地区的旧房子。

Experts advise the government to demolish the old houses
in the downtown area.

aftermath ['æftərmæθ]

释义· *n.* （灾难性事件的）后果；余波

例句· 经济衰退以及其造成的后果已经使一些高龄工作者破产。

The recession and its aftermath have already pushed down
some older workers.

contemporary [kən'tempəreri]

释义· *adj.* 当代的；同一时代的 *n.* 同时代的人

例句· 在当代社会，人们的信仰和现实之间的冲突越来越激烈。

In contemporary society, the conflict between people's faith
and reality is becoming more and more intense.

welfare ['welfer]

释义· *n.* (U) 福利；幸福

例句· 这个社区中的多数人都是靠救济生活。

Most of the people in this neighborhood are on welfare.

搭配· 社会福利 social welfare

公共福利 public welfare

接受救济的 on welfare

curtail [kɜːr'teɪl]

释义· *vt.* 缩减；减少；限制

例句· 北约计划缩减派往该地区的士兵数量。

NATO plans to curtail the number of troops being sent to the region.

派生· curtailment *n.* 减缩；缩短；限制

搭配· 缩减开支 curtail expenditure

poverty ['pɑːvərti]

释义· *n.* (U) 贫困；贫穷

例句· 我们需要制定一个有效的对策来与贫困作斗争。

We need an effective strategy to fight poverty.

搭配· 贫困线 the poverty line

贫困；处于贫困当中 in poverty

immigrate ['ɪmɪɡreɪt]

释义· *v.* （从外国）移居；作为移民定居

例句· 接下来的两年里预计有10000人会移民至此。

10,000 people are expected to immigrate in the next two years.

派生· immigrant *n.* 移民；侨民

immigration *n.* 移居（入境）

norms [nɔːrms]

释义· *n.* (pl.) 规范；行为标准

例句· 所采取的这些行动背离了她所谓的那些普遍接受的民主准则。

The actions taken depart from what she called the commonly accepted norms of democracy.

搭配· 社会规范 social norms

criterion [kraɪ'tɪriən]

释义· *n.* （判断、决定）的标准；准则

例句· 我们挑选候选人的标准是他们必须有至少10年的执政经验。

The criteria we use to select candidates is that they must
have at least ten years' governing experience.

搭配· 道德规范；道德准则 moral criterion

扩展· criteria (*pl.*)

community [kə'mjuːnəti]

释义· *n.* 社区；群体；团体

例句· 社区领导人见面讨论拟建高尔夫球场一事。
Community leaders met to discuss the proposed golf course.

搭配· 国际社会 the international community
社区学院 community college
社区中心 community center
邻里意识 sense of community

gamble ['gæmbl]

释义· *v.* 冒险；赌博；投机 *n.* 冒险；投机；赌博

例句· 昨天他冒了很大的风险任命了内阁成员。
Yesterday, he named his cabinet and took a big gamble in
the process.

派生· gambler *n.* 赌徒；投机者

搭配· 以某物为某事的赌注 gamble sth. on sth.
赌光 gamble away

augment [ɔːg'ment]

释义· *v.* 增加；增大；提高

例句· 凯西说，除了国际社会采取的措施之外，美国也可能增加新的
制裁。
Casey said in addition to measures taken by the
international community, the United States could augment

sanctions.

派生 · augmentation *n.* 增加；增大

shield [ʃiːld]

释义 · *v.* 保护；掩护 *n.* 盾牌；保护物

例句 · 政府征收进口关税以保护本国企业不受外国竞争威胁。

The government levies import tariffs that shield firms from foreign competition.

搭配 · 保护某人 / 某物免遭…… shield sb./sth. from sb./sth.

intricate ['ɪntrɪkət]

释义 · *adj.* 错综复杂的

例句 · 在这种错综复杂的经济形势下，该国人民的命运取决于政府的政策能否解决问题。

In this intricate economic situation, the fate of the people depends on whether the government's policies can solve the problem.

派生 · intricacy *n.* 复杂精细；错综复杂

district ['dɪstrɪkt]

释义 · *n.* 地区；区域；行政区

例句 · 这个地区的大部分建筑归政府所有。

Most buildings in this district belong to the government.

搭配 · 市区　urban district

　　　商务区　business district

　　　居住区　residential district

　　　工业区　industrial district

ubiquitous [juːˈbɪkwɪtəs]

释义 · *adj.* 无所不在的；随处可见的

例句· 新的规则增强了对非政府组织外国资金的监督，这便是政府监督是无处不在的例子。

The new regulations increasing oversight of foreign funding for Chinese NGOs is an example of how ubiquitous government oversight is.

colonize [ˈkɑːlənaɪz]

释义· v. 在（某国家或地区）建立殖民地；（动植物）在（某一地区）聚居

例句· 英国最早尝试在爱尔兰开拓殖民地是在 12 世纪。

The first British attempt to colonize Ireland was in the twelfth century.

同根· colonial adj. 殖民国家的；殖民的

colonist n. 殖民地定居者

defense [dɪˈfens]

释义· n. 防御；保卫；国防

例句· 所以，我们将继续努力说服俄罗斯，我们需要在导弹防御系统问题上密切合作。

So we will continue to make the case to Russia that we need to cooperate closely on missile defense.

同根· defenseless adj. 无防御的

defensive adj. 防御的；自卫的

搭配· 国防 national defense

防御某物 defense against sth.

为保卫…… in defense of

advocate [ˈædvəkeɪt]

释义· vt. 主张；提倡；拥护

例句 · 威廉斯先生是个保守派，主张政府应减少对商业的控制。

Mr. Williams is a conservative who advocates fewer government controls on business.

pressing ['presɪŋ]

释义 · *adj.* 紧迫的；迫切的 *n.* 模压制品

例句 · 在非洲贫困是一个比污染更紧迫的问题。

Poverty is a more pressing problem than pollution in Africa.

搭配 · 紧急问题 pressing issues

slogan ['sloʊgən]

释义 · *n.* 标语；口号

例句 · "这是一场全体人民的革命。"一副普通的标语上写道。

"This is the revolution of all the people, " read a common slogan.

policy ['pɑːləsi]

释义 · *n.* 政策；方针；策略；保险单

例句 · 当他开始解释他的政策时，人们嘘叫着表示反对。

People hooted at the speaker when he began to explain his policy.

搭配 · 外交政策 foreign policy

财政政策 fiscal policy

infrastructure ['ɪnfrəstrʌktʃər]

释义 · *n.* 基础设施

例句 · 一些国家缺乏适当的经济基础设施。

Some countries lack a suitable economic infrastructure.

搭配 · 基础设施建设 infrastructure construction

shrink [ʃrɪŋk]

释义· v. (使) 缩小，收缩；畏缩 n. 精神病学家；心理学家

例句· 匈牙利可能不得不降低其压缩国有企业的预期。

Hungary may have to lower its hopes of shrinking its state sector.

搭配· 畏避（做）某事　shrink from (doing) sth.

因害怕而退缩　shrink back

扩展· shrank/shrunk (过去式) shrunk (过去分词)

circulation [ˌsɜːrkjəˈleɪʃn]

释义· n. 流通；流传；(报刊) 发行量

例句· 在像美国这样的社会里，可能有 1.8 亿支枪在民间。

In a society like America, there are perhaps 180 million guns in circulation.

同根· circulate v. 循环；传播；流传

circulating adj. 循环的；流通的

thrive [θraɪv]

释义· vi. 繁荣；兴旺发达；茁壮成长

例句· 只有这样，我们才能继续繁荣昌盛，为所有人建设一个更美好的家园。

Only then can we continue to thrive, and build a better homeland for all.

派生· thriving adj. 繁荣的；兴旺的

搭配· 以某事为乐（尤指别人不喜欢的事物）thrive on sth.

扩展· throve (过去式) thriven (过去分词)

demonstrate [ˈdemənstreɪt]

释义· v. 进行示威游行（或集会）；证明；论证

例句 · 在城市里，大批的人群举行示威游行，要求进行变革。

In the cities, vast crowds have been demonstrating for change.

派生 · demonstration *n.* 游行示威；示范；证明

搭配 · 示威游行反对某事 demonstrate against sth.

示威游行支持某事 demonstrate in favor/support of sth.

impose [ɪm'poʊz]

释义 · *v.* 强制实行；把（看法、信仰）强加（于……）

例句 · 法庭可以强制执行罚款。

The court can impose a fine.

派生 · imposition *n.* 强制实行

搭配 · 把某事物强加于某人 / 某物 impose sth. on/upon sb./sth.

处以罚款 impose a fine

resource ['riːsɔːrs]

释义 · *n.* 资源；财力 *v.* 向……提供资金（或设备）

例句 · 中国是一个自然资源丰富的国家。

China is a country rich in natural resources.

派生 · resourceful *adj.* 足智多谋的；机智的

搭配 · 自然资源 natural resource

可再生资源 renewable resource

population [ˌpɑːpjuˈleɪʃn]

释义 · *n.* （某一国家或地区的）全体人民，人口

例句 · 在接下来的 20 年里，该地区的城市人口将增加一倍以上。

The region's urban population will more than double in the next two decades.

搭配 · 人口稠密的 densely-populated

人口密度　population density

人口激增；人口爆炸　population explosion

civilized ['sɪvəlaɪzd]

释义· *adj.* 文明的；有礼貌的

例句· 这种事情不应该发生在文明社会。

Such things should not happen in a civilized society.

同根· civilization *n.* 文明；文明世界

搭配· 文明社会　civilized society

regulation [ˌregju'leɪʃn]

释义· *n.* 条例；规则；管理

例句· 地方当局正在引入新的规划条例。

The local authority is introducing new planning regulations.

搭配· 交通规则　traffic regulation

havoc ['hævək]

释义· *n.* (U) 大混乱；大破坏

例句· 罢工将给乘车上下班的人造成混乱。

A strike will cause havoc for commuters.

搭配· 造成严重破坏　wreak havoc

严重破坏　play havoc with

maintain [meɪn'teɪn]

释义· *v.* 保持；维持；维修；坚持（意见）

例句· 英国希望保持其作为世界强国的地位。

Britain wants to maintain its position as a world power.

搭配· 维护世界和平　maintain world peace

jeopardize ['dʒepərdaɪz]

释义 · *vt.* 危及；危害；损害

例句 · 他的行为已经危及他这届政府的未来。

He has jeopardized the future of his administration.

awareness [ə'wernəs]

释义 · *n.* (U) 认识；意识；明白

例句 · 卫生部官员们试图提高人们对艾滋病的认识。

Health officials have tried to raise awareness about AIDS.

reform [rɪ'fɔːrm]

释义 · *n.* 改革；变革 *v.* 改革；改良；(使) 改过自新

例句 · 这个党开始进行经济改革。

The party embarked on a programme of economic reform.

搭配 · reform and opening-up 改革开放

ethic ['eθɪk]

释义 · *n.* 道德规范；伦理标准

例句 · 旧有的崇尚勤勉的道德观已被及时行乐的新观念所取代。

The old ethic of hard work has given way to a new ethic of instant gratification.

派生 · ethical *adj.* 伦理的；道德的

搭配 · 社会伦理；社会道德 social ethic

职业道德 professional ethic

bribe [braɪb]

释义 · *v.* 向……行贿 *n.* 贿赂

例句 · 他被指控贿赂一名高级银行官员。

He was accused of bribing a senior bank official.

派生· bribery *n.* 行贿；贿赂

搭配· 买通某人做某事 bribe sb. to do sth.

用某物贿赂某人 bribe sb. with sth.

implement ['ɪmplɪment]

释义· *vt.* 实施；执行；使生效 *n.* 工具；器具

例句· 政府许诺实施新的制度来控制金融贷款机构。

The government promised to implement a new system to control financial loan institutions.

搭配· 执行计划；实施计划 implement plan

实施改革 implement reforms

释义	短语
加大对……的投入	increase the inputs in
一个国家的民众	the populace of a country
电网	power grid
引起很大关注	catch much attention
对坏事负有责任	be to blame for sth.
犯罪率上升	a rising crime rate
优化资源配置	optimize the distribution of resource
长期问题	long-term problem
医疗保健	health care
转移资金做某事	divert money to do sth.
政府在某事物上的支出	government's spending/expenditure on sth.
在……和……之间找到一种平衡	strike a balance between...and...
执法	enforce the law
阶级两极分化	class polarization
对……优先考虑	give precedence to
白手起家；从头做起	from scratch

社会福祉	social well-being
恶性循环	a vicious circle
熔炉	melting pot
给……特别的关照	give special care to
国家非物质遗产	national intangible heritage
社会动荡	social instability
扩大 / 缩小两者之间的差距	widen/narrow the gap between...and...
城市建设	urban construction
采取一些预防 / 补救措施	take some preventive/remedial measures

巩固练习

练习1 根据下面的中文释义，写出对应的单词（词组）。

A

民主 d_____

条例 r_____

当代的 c_____

根基 f_____

福利 w_____

医疗保健 h_____

危及 j_____

禁止 p_____

事件 i_____

先决条件 p_____

城市建设 u_____

B

后果 a_____

详细阐明 e_____

恶性循环 a_____

道德规范 e_____

基础设施 i_____

保持 m_____

拆毁 d_____

预算 b_____

严格的 s_____

错综复杂的 i_____

强制实行 i_____

练习2 用方框中所给单词（词组）的适当形式填空。

exaggerate	abolish	interfere in	declare	establish
aggravate	exclude	undergo	curtail	bribe
tackle	shield	emerge	thrive	demolish

1. These reforms will a_____（废除）racially discriminatory laws.

2. The government's goal is to e_____（建立）a new research center in the North.

3. The government is determined to t_____ (解决) inflation.

4. But out of it will e_____ (出现) an economy where Made in China is not just sold abroad, but bought at home too.

5. Governments often e_____ (夸大) some data or facts to gain widespread support.

6. The country has u_____ (经历) massive changes recently.

7. Their money problems were further a_____ (使严重) by a rise in interest rates.

8. The UN cannot i_____ (干涉) the internal affairs of any country.

9. Women are still e_____ (阻止……参加) from some London clubs.

10. He d_____ (声明) he would not run for a second term as president.

11. Experts advise the government to d_____ (拆毁) the old houses in the downtown area.

12. NATO plans to c_____ (缩减) the number of troops being sent to the region.

13. The government levies import tariffs that s_____ (保护) firms from foreign competition.

14. Only then can we continue to t_____ (繁荣), and build a better homeland for all.

15. He was accused of b_____ (向……行贿) a senior bank official.

☐ abolish	☐ forbid	☐ subsidy
☐ legalize	☐ majority	☐ democracy
☐ boom	☐ collapse	☐ virtue
☐ deteriorate	☐ legislation	☐ corrupt
☐ crisis	☐ conservative	☐ interfere
☐ broadcast	☐ substantiate	☐ intrusion
☐ reinforce	☐ exaggerate	☐ municipal
☐ disrupt	☐ urge	☐ stringent
☐ establish	☐ delinquency	☐ citizen
☐ circumstance	☐ publicity	☐ hierarchy
☐ plague	☐ inevitable	☐ exclude
☐ prohibit	☐ combat	☐ distribution
☐ dispose	☐ estate	☐ devastate
☐ coexist	☐ metropolis	☐ ban
☐ enact	☐ survey	☐ ideology
☐ penalty	☐ foundation	☐ principle
☐ bureaucracy	☐ undergo	☐ conceal
☐ tackle	☐ beneficiary	☐ scrutiny
☐ incident	☐ revenue	☐ individual
☐ prerequisite	☐ proportion	☐ allocate
☐ dominate	☐ aggravate	☐ declare
☐ congress	☐ fiscal	☐ investment
☐ guidance	☐ commit	☐ entitle
☐ emerge	☐ influential	☐ flourish

☐ security	☐ augment	☐ impose
☐ budget	☐ shield	☐ resource
☐ expand	☐ intricate	☐ population
☐ confine	☐ district	☐ civilized
☐ demolish	☐ ubiquitous	☐ regulation
☐ aftermath	☐ colonize	☐ havoc
☐ contemporary	☐ defense	☐ maintain
☐ welfare	☐ advocate	☐ jeopardize
☐ curtail	☐ slogan	☐ awareness
☐ poverty	☐ policy	☐ reform
☐ immigrate	☐ infrastructure	☐ ethic
☐ norms	☐ shrink	☐ bribe
☐ criterion	☐ circulation	☐ implement
☐ community	☐ thrive	
☐ gamble	☐ demonstrate	

表中共有 115 个单词

您不确认的单词 _____ 个，占总数的 _____%

如果比例高于 10%，请耐心再复习一遍。如果比例低于 10%，您可以开始下一章的托福写作之旅了！

第七章

科学技术

advanced [əd'vænst]

释义· *adj.* 先进的；高级的；高龄的

例句· 与美国等发达国家相比，中国的农业生产率仍然较低。

Agricultural productivity of China remained low by comparison with advanced countries like the United States.

搭配· 先进技术　advanced technology

高等数学　Advanced Mathematics

高等教育　advanced education

dimension [daɪ'menʃn]

释义· *n.* （数）维；方面；尺寸

例句· 这部电影的画面是三维的。

The frames of this film are in three dimensions.

abundance [ə'bʌndəns]

释义· *n.* (U) 丰富；充裕

例句· 食物种类的丰富得益于生产和加工技术的发展。

The abundance of food owes to the development of

manufacture and processing technology.

搭配· 大量；丰盛；充裕 in abundance

utilize ['juːtəlaɪz]

释义· *vt.* 运用；利用

例句· 音响师运用一系列技术来提高录音质量。

Sound engineers utilize a range of techniques to enhance

the quality of the recordings.

派生· utilization *n.* 利用；使用

utilizer *n.* 应用者

utilizable *adj.* 可利用的

搭配· 用于…… utilize for

scientific [ˌsaɪən'tɪfɪk]

释义· *adj.* 科学的；细致严谨的

例句· 科学研究被普遍认为是美国高生活水准的源泉。

Scientific research is widely claimed to be the source of the

high standard of living in the US.

派生· scientifically *adv.* 科学地；合乎科学地

display [dɪ'spleɪ]

释义· *v.* 显示；表现；炫耀 *n.* 陈列；显示

例句· 他们开始在显示那些图像的电脑屏幕上寻找。

They started out by looking at the computer screens which

display the images.

搭配· 陈列；展出 on display

数字显示 digital display

图像显示 image display

dramatic [drə'mætɪk]

释义· *adj.* 巨大的；急剧的；引人注目的；戏剧的

例句· 人工智能技术将给各行各业带来巨大的变化。

AI technology will bring dramatic changes to various jobs.

functional ['fʌŋkʃənl]

释义· *adj.* （机器等）工作的，运转的；功能的；实用的

例句· 一些人预测，到 2020 年，无人驾驶汽车将全面投入使用。

Some predict that driverless cars will be fully functional by 2020.

派生· functionally *adv.* 功能上地

cyber ['saɪbər]

释义· *adj.* 网络的；计算机的

例句· 奥巴马说，网络安全和知识产权保护是他希望讨论的两个问题。

Cyber-security and the protection of intellectual property rights were two areas the president said he wants to discuss.

合成· cyberspace *n.* 网络空间

搭配· 网络犯罪 cyber crime

milestone ['maɪlstoʊn]

释义· *n.* 里程碑；重大事件

例句· 电灯的发明是第二次工业革命的里程碑。

The invention of the electric lamp is the milestone of the second industrial revolution.

surpass [sərˈpæs]

释义· *v.* 超过；胜过；优于

例句· 一些科学家担心人工智能在未来会超过人类的智商。

Some scientists are worried about that AI will surpass the IQ of the human being in the future.

派生· surpassing *adj.* 胜过的；卓越的

antibiotics [ˌæntibaɪˈɑːtɪks]

释义· *n.* 抗生素；抗菌素

例句· 即使在像比利时和法国等已减少使用抗生素的西欧国家，滥用仍在继续。

Even in western Europe, where countries such as Belgium and France have reduced the use of antibiotics, misuse continues.

antithetical [ˌæntɪˈθetɪkl]

释义· *adj.* 对立的；相反的

例句· 有时你会发现有些发明的功能与发明者的初衷完全相反。

Sometimes you may find that the functions of some inventions are entirely antithetical to the original intention of inventors.

搭配· 与……相反；和……对立 be antithetical to

对立的观点 antithetical idea

commercialized [kəˈmɜːrʃəlaɪzd]

释义· *adj.* 商业化的

例句· 许多公司在追求把太空旅行商业化。

Many companies are pursuing commercialized space travel.

vehicle ['vi:əkl]

释义· *n.* 车辆；交通工具；媒介

例句· 这种车辆采用了一项最新的技术来确保安全性。

This kind of vehicle adopted one latest technique to guarantee safety.

搭配· 赖以表达思想、感情或达到目的的手段、工具 vehicle for sth.

汽车尾气 vehicle exhaust

扩展	释义	单词	释义	单词
	汽车	automobile	特快列车	express
	四轮马车	carriage	吉普车	jeep
	运货马车	cart	混合动力车	hybrid car
	长途汽车；长途客车	coach	私家车	private car

malicious [mə'lɪʃəs]

释义· *adj.* 怀有恶意的；恶毒的

例句· 许多手机安装了一些用户无法删除的恶意软件。

Many cellphones were installed some malicious software that user cannot delete.

派生· maliciousness *n.* 恶意

deterioration [dɪ,tɪriə'reɪʃn]

释义· *n.* 退化；恶化

例句· 过多的高科技产品有可能导致人类思维能力的退化。

Too many high-tech products are likely to cause the deterioration of human's thinking ability.

overcrowded [,oʊvər'kraʊdɪd]

释义· *adj.* 过度拥挤的

例句· 这项技术有助于缓解上海等华南拥挤城市的"城市热岛效应"。
This technique could help relieve the "urban heat island effect" in the overcrowded cities of Southern China, such as Shanghai.

gravity ['grævəti]

释义· *n.* (U) 重力；地球引力；（事态的）严重性
例句· 重力的作用随着距离的增大而减小，但是不可能完全消失。
The effect of gravity diminishes with distance, but it never truly goes away.
同根· gravitate *vi.* 被吸引到；受吸引而转向

track [træk]

释义· *v.* 追踪；跟踪 *n.* 小道；足迹；轨道
例句· 这款应用可以追踪用户的数据，从而更好地为客户服务。
This APP can track down the users' data to better serve the clients.
派生· tracker *n.* 追踪装置
trackable *adj.* 可追踪的
搭配· 查到；追踪到 track down
稳步前进；做法对头 be on track
思路对头 / 不对头 on the right/wrong track
田径 track and field

boundary ['baʊndri]

释义· *n.* （学科或活动的）界限，边界；（土地的）分界线，边界
例句· 新技术正在不断扩大人类知识的范围。
The new technology is continuously extending the boundaries of human knowledge.
搭配· 边缘科学 boundary science

overshadow [ˌoʊvərˈʃædoʊ]

释义· *vt.* 给……蒙上阴影；使黯然失色

例句· 苹果的 iOS 和谷歌的安卓系统的出现使得诺基亚的塞班系统黯然失色。

The advent of Apple's iOS and Google's Android overshadowed Nokia's Symbian OS.

hazard [ˈhæzərd]

释义· *n.* 危险；危害 *vt.* 冒……的风险；斗胆提出

例句· 任何的科学研究都有失败的风险，但在失败中探索正是科学精神之所在。

Every scientific research has the hazard of failure, however, to explore in defeat is the spirit of science.

派生· hazardous *adj.* 危险的；有害的

搭配· 侥幸的；在危机中 in hazard

冒一切危险；不惜任何代价 at all hazards

curb [kɜːrb]

释义· *vt.* 抑制；控制；限定 *n.* 起控制（或限制）作用的事物

例句· 俄罗斯需要抑制通货膨胀。

Inflation needs to be curbed in Russia.

搭配· 保持对……的控制 keep a curb on

apparatus [ˌæpəˈrætəs]

释义· *n.* 设备；装置；器官；机构

例句· 这整个装置可以被安置在不超过几平方毫米的芯片上。

This entire apparatus fits on a chip no larger than a few square millimeters.

扩展· apparatuses (*pl.*)

redundant [rɪ'dʌndənt]

释义· *adj.* 多余的；不需要的；（人）被裁减的

例句· 技术上的革新可能意味着曾经被重视的技术现在已变得多余。

Changes in technology may mean that once-valued skills are now redundant.

搭配· 超额人员　redundant staff

replicate ['replɪkeɪt]

释义· *v.* 复制；重做

例句· 这款新产品不仅复制了上代的主要功能，还使用了最新的操作系统。

This new product not only replicates the primary function of the previous generation but also use the latest operating system.

派生· replication *n.* 复制

span [spæn]

释义· *n.* 持续时间；跨度；范围　*vt.* 跨越；持续

例句· 这款锂电池会延长手机的使用寿命，而且充电速度更快。

This lithium battery will extend the life span of cellphone and accelerate battery charging.

搭配· 在……期间；在……范围内　over/within/in a span of sth.

寿命；使用期限　life span

时间跨度　time span

扩展· spanned（过去式）spanned（过去分词）

invent [ɪn'vent]

释义· *vt.* 发明；创造；虚构

例句· 电话是亚历山大·格雷厄姆·贝尔发明的。

The telephone was invented by Alexander Graham Bell.

派生 · inventor *n.* 发明家

invention *n.* 发明；发明物

accelerate [ək'seləreɪt]

释义 · v. (使)加速，加快

例句 · 由于这个原因，网络技术将会加强这个网络时代的"自然规律"，并加速它的进程，而这一切都只是时间问题。

For that reason, it was only a matter of time until the technologies of the network would reinforce this natural tendency, and accelerate it.

反义 · decelerate *v.* (使)减速行驶

派生 · accelerated *adj.* 加速的

accelerating *adj.* 促进的；催化的

transportation [ˌtrænspɔːr'teɪʃn]

释义 · n. (U) 运输；交通运输系统；交通工具

例句 · 他们还大幅削减了对公共事业和交通运输的政府补贴。

They've also slashed state subsidies to utilities and transportation.

搭配 · 运输业 the transportation industry

公共交通运输系统 public transportation

城市交通运输系统 urban transportation

artificial [ˌɑːrtɪ'fɪʃl]

释义 · adj. 人工的；人造的；虚假的

例句 · 我们计算机科学系有讨论人工智能的课程。

We have classes that discuss artificial intelligence within the computer science department.

派生· artificiality *n.* 人工；人造物

搭配· 人工智能　artificial intelligence

compute [kəmˈpjuːt]

释义· *v.* 计算；估算

例句· 计算机可以在几秒钟内计算出这个复杂的方程。

Computers can compute this complex equation within seconds.

派生· computerize *vt.* 用计算机做；使计算机化

mass [mæs]

释义· *adj.* 大批的；数量极多的 *n.* 大量；质量；块 *v.* 聚集

例句· 工厂流水线的应用使得大规模生产成为可能。

The application of the factory's assembly lines makes it possible for mass production.

派生· massive *adj.* 大量的；巨大的

搭配· 群众　the masses

大众文化　mass culture

批量生产　mass production

大量的　a mass of

总体上，总的来说　in the mass

alternative [ɔːlˈtɜːrnətɪv]

释义· *adj.*（能源）替代的，代用的 *n.* 可供选择的事物

例句· 各国都在研发新的技术以寻找替代能源。

Countries are developing new technologies to find alternative sources of energy.

搭配· 替代能源　alternative energy

别无选择　have no alternative

exploration [ˌeksplə'reɪʃn]

释义· *n.* 探索；探究

例句· 想象一下，你的朋友将要乘坐宇宙飞船去探索木星或者其他的什么东西。

Just imagine your friend is about to go on the spaceship which is going to do the exploration of Jupiter or whatever.

同根· explorer *n.* 探险家；探险者

fantasy ['fæntəsi]

释义· *n.* 幻想；想象

例句· 新技术的出现使得小说中描绘的情景不再是幻想。

The new technology makes the scenes described in the fiction no longer a fantasy.

同根· fantastic *adj.* 极好的；了不起的

fantasize *v.* 幻想

convey [kən'veɪ]

释义· *v.* 传达；运输

例句· 当我们通过互联网传递信息时是非常方便的。

It is very convenient when we convey information via the Internet.

派生· conveyance *n.* 运输；交通工具

conveyor *n.* 传送者；运送者

搭配· 传达某物给某人 convey sth. to sb.

automatic [ˌɔːtə'mætɪk]

释义· *adj.* 自动的；无意识的；必然的 *n.* 自动枪

例句· 自动存储会自动增加数据库在磁盘和文件系统上的大小。

Automatic storage automatically grows the size of your

database across disk and file systems.

同根· automate *v.* 使自动化

搭配· 自动驾驶　automatic drive

全自动的　fully automatic

substitute ['sʌbstɪtuːt]

释义· *n.* 替代品；替代者 *v.* 用……代替；取代

例句· 天然气是一种很好的煤的替代品，干净又廉价。

Natural gas, clean and cheap, is a good substitute for coal.

派生· substitution *n.* 代替；代替物

搭配· 替代某人 / 某物　substitute for sb./sth.

某物不可替代（形容特别重要）be no substitute for sth.

innovation [ˌɪnəˈveɪʃn]

释义· *n.* 革新；创新

例句· 许多人对技术革新的速度感到不知所措。

Many people feel bewildered by the speed of technological innovation.

同根· innovative *adj.* 新颖的

innovational *adj.* 创新的；富有革新精神的

搭配· 技术革新　technological innovation

创新能力　innovation ability

derive [dɪˈraɪv]

释义· *v.* 获得；取得；（使）起源于

例句· 从医学的角度来讲，这一技术将使我们受益匪浅。

Medically, we will derive great benefit from this technique.

派生· derivation *n.* 起源；由来；（尤指）词源

搭配· 起源于 / 来自某物　derive from sth./be derived from sth.

infinite ['ɪnfɪnət]

释义· *adj.* 无限的；无穷的 *n.* 无限的事物

例句· 随着获得的知识越来越多，我们就越明白宇宙是无限的。

With the more knowledge we obtain, we realize that the universe is infinite.

派生· infinitesimal *adj.* 极小的 *n.* 无穷小

unprecedented [ʌn'presɪdentɪd]

释义· *adj.* 前所未有的；空前的；没有先例的

例句· 大数据与人工智能的结合将给人类带来前所未有的改变。

The marriage of big data and AI will bring the unprecedented changes for the human.

static ['stætɪk]

释义· *adj.* 静态的；静止的

例句· 在系统内，静态结构通过显示类型和它们的实例进行传播。

Static structure is conveyed by showing the types and their instances in the system.

反义· dynamic *adj.* 动态的；充满活力的

operation [,ɑːpə'reɪʃn]

释义· *n.* 操作；运算；手术

例句· 在计算机的帮助下，这台机器操作起来很简单。

With the help of the computer, the operation of this machine is straightforward.

同根· operational *adj.* 操作的；运转的

operative *adj.* 起作用的；运转着的

搭配· 工作中；使用中；有效 in operation

动手术 have an operation

dense [dens]

释义· *adj.* 密集的；稠密的；浓厚的；愚笨的
例句· 因此，空间站的雷达图像看起来就像一个密集的光点集合。
The radar image of the station therefore looks like a dense collection of bright spots.
派生· density *n.* 密度
搭配· 人口密集地区 areas of dense population

appliance [ə'plaɪəns]

释义· *n.* （家用）电器，器械，装置
例句· 当按下按钮重新启动设备时，它会回到待机状态。
When the appliance is reactivated by pressing a button, it goes back into standby mode.
搭配· 电器 electrical appliance

launch [lɔːntʃ]

释义· *v.* 发射；发动；开始从事 *n.* 发射；上市
例句· 美国国家航空航天局计划发射一颗卫星上天，对宇宙射线进行研究。
NASA plans to launch a satellite to study cosmic rays.
搭配· （热情地）开始做某事 launch into sth.
开始从事，投身于（新的、尤指更令人兴奋的事业）launch out

mitigate ['mɪtɪgeɪt]

释义· *v.* 减轻；缓和
例句· 需要采取措施来减轻燃煤增加对环境造成的影响。
Measures need to be taken to mitigate the environmental effects of burning more coal.
派生· mitigation *n.* 减轻；缓和

perpetual [pər'petʃuəl]

释义· *adj.* 永久的；不间断的

例句· 任何高科技都造不出永动机，因为它违背了科学原理。

No high-tech can produce perpetual mobile because it violates the scientific principle.

soar [sɔːr]

释义· *v.* 猛增；高飞；高涨；耸立

例句· 因为互联网的缘故，数据猛增，信息爆炸，生活节奏加快。

Because of the Internet, data is soaring, information is exploding, and the pace of life is speeding up.

派生· soaring *adj.* 猛增的；高耸的；翱翔的

explosion [ɪk'sploʊʒn]

释义· *n.* 爆发；爆炸；激增

例句· 许多电脑专家正在处理最近爆发的电脑病毒。

Many computer experts are dealing with the recent explosion of a computer virus.

同根· explosive *adj.* 易爆炸的；爆炸性的 *n.* 炸药

staggering ['stægərɪŋ]

释义· *adj.* 令人大吃一惊的；令人震惊的

例句· 近年来，中国互联网速度的增长令人咂舌。

In recent years, China has experienced the staggering rise of the Internet speed.

cozy ['koʊzi]

释义· *adj.* 温暖舒适的；亲密无间的；愉快的

例句· 他们希望确保客人们感到舒适温暖。

They like to make sure their guests are comfortable and cozy.

搭配· 向某人献殷勤 cozy up to sb.

breakthrough ['breɪkθruː]

释义· *n.* 突破；重大进展

例句· 科学家在癌症治疗方面取得了重大突破。

Scientists have made a breakthrough in the treatment of cancer.

搭配· 作出 / 取得突破性进展 make/achieve a breakthrough

virtual ['vɜːrtʃuəl]

释义· *adj.* 虚拟的；事实上的

例句· 虚拟现实技术使我们无法区分真假。

The technology of virtual reality makes us fail to distinguish the real and fake.

派生· virtually *adv.* 事实上；几乎

搭配· 虚拟现实 virtual reality (VR)

investigate [ɪn'vestɪɡeɪt]

释义· *v.* 调查；研究

例句· 那个计算能力将用于调查天文学中一些最大的悬而未决的问题。

That power will be used to investigate some of the biggest outstanding questions in astronomy.

同义· check into/inquire into 调查

派生· investigation *n.* 调查

terminate ['tɜːrmɪneɪt]

释义· *v.* 结束；终止

例句· 有人说人类历史将被人工智能终结。

Someone says that the human history will be terminated by artificial intelligence.

派生· termination *n.* 结束；终止

global ['gloʊbl]

释义· *adj.* 全球的；整体的

例句· 将会出现一个电话、电脑、电视互动的真正的地球村。
There will be a true global village in which telephones, computers and televisions interact.

同根· globalization *n.* 全球化
globalize *v.* （使）全球化

搭配· 全球变暖 global warming

revolution [ˌrevə'luːʃn]

释义· *n.* 革命；旋转

例句· 我们近年来看到的房地产繁荣在多大程度上是金融技术革命的结果？
To what extent was the housing boom that we saw in recent years the result of the revolution in financial technology?

同根· revolutionary *adj.* 革命的；突破性的
revolutionize *vt.* 彻底改变；完全变革

搭配· 工业革命 Industrial Revolution

dominant ['dɑːmɪnənt]

释义· *adj.* 占支配（或统治）地位的；占优势的；显著的

例句· 日本是亚洲进口货物和技术的最大供应国。
Japan is Asia's dominant supplier of imports and technology.

派生· dominance *n.* 控制；支配

搭配· 统治地位；支配地位 dominant position

主要角色 dominant role

novel ['nɑːvl]

释义· *adj.* 新奇的；新颖的 *n.* （长篇）小说

例句· 随着科学技术的快速发展，每天都有新奇的事物出现。

With the rapid development of science and technology, something novel happens every day.

派生· novelty *n.* 新奇；新奇的事物

renewable [rɪ'nuːəbl]

释义· *adj.* 可再生的；可更新的

例句· 我们应该推广可再生能源的使用，比如风能、太阳能和生物质能等。

We should advertise to use renewable energy, like putting up wind and solar and biomasses, et cetera.

搭配· 可再生资源 renewable resource

extinction [ɪk'stɪŋkʃn]

释义· *n.* 消亡；消灭；（物种的）灭绝

例句· 无人驾驶汽车的出现意味着司机这个职业的消亡。

The emergence of the pilotless automobile means the extinction of drivers.

搭配· 濒临灭绝 on the verge/edge/brink of extinction

probe [proʊb]

释义· *n.* 探测（器）；调查 *v.* 探测；调查；探究

例句· 它的圆环是从地球上用望远镜发现的，但是太空探测器后来又发现了围绕其他一些星球的壮观的圆环。

Its rings were discovered by telescope from Earth, but space probes later found that spectacular rings surround some other planets.

搭配 · 探究某物 probe into sth.

航天探测器；宇宙探测航天器 space probe

update [ˌʌpˈdeɪt]

释义 · *vt.* 更新；使现代化

例句 · 您将使用这些命令来创建、读取、更新或者删除数据库中的记录。

You will use these commands to create, read, update, or delete records from your database.

派生 · update *n.* 最新消息；快讯；速递

搭配 · 向某人提供最新信息 update sb. on sth.

supersede [ˌsuːpərˈsiːd]

释义 · *vt.* 取代，替代（陈旧或令人不满意的事物）

例句 · 手工工具是历史的遗物，现在已经被机器所取代。

Hand tools are relics of the past that have now been superseded by the machine.

assemble [əˈsembl]

释义 · *v.* 组装；装配；集合；聚集

例句 · 汽车由成千上万个部件组成，每个部件都有特定的功能。

A car is assembled by thousands of parts each of which has unique function.

反义 · disassemble *vt.* 拆卸；拆开

派生 · assembly *n.* 装配；组装

paradise [ˈpærədaɪs]

释义 · *n.* 天堂；乐土

例句 · 人们期待着在高科技的帮助下，未来我们可以在地球上建造一个人间天堂。

People are looking forward to the future that we can build a paradise on earth with the help of high technology.

搭配· 做黄粱美梦；生活在幻想世界 live in a fool's paradise

productive [prə'dʌktɪv]

释义· *adj.* 多产的；生产的；富有成效的

例句· 我们要做的是提高生产效率，而唯一的方法就是推动科技创新。
What we have to do is become a lot more productive, and the only way is to promote scientific and technological innovation.

同根· productivity *n.* 生产力
productively *adv.* 有结果地；有成果地

搭配· 生产能力 productive capacity

converge [kən'vɜːrdʒ]

释义· *v.* 汇聚；汇合；趋同

例句· 这台机器融合了最新的操作系统、最新的科研成果和最时尚的设计。
This machine converges the latest OS and scientific payoffs and the most fashionable design.

反义· diverge *v.* 分歧；分化

派生· convergent *adj.* 趋同的；会合的
convergence *n.* 趋同；融合

搭配· 汇聚…… converge on

hack [hæk]

释义· *v.* 非法侵入（他人计算机系统）；砍；劈

例句· 有人非法侵入了这家公司的中心数据库。
Somebody hacked into the company's central database.

派生· hacker *n.* 黑客

搭配· 侵入某物 hack into sth.

simulate ['sɪmjuleɪt]

释义· *vt.*（用计算机或模型等）模拟；模仿；假装

例句· 计算机科学研究利用计算机模拟人类思维。

Computer science deals with using computers to simulate human thinking.

派生· simulation *n.* 模拟；假装

simulated *adj.* 模拟的；假装的

simulator *n.* 模拟装置

transform [træns'fɔːrm]

释义· *v.* 转换；改变；改造

例句· 风、水和太阳都可以转化为电能，而且这些资源是无限的。

Wind, water and sun can be transformed into electricity, and these resources are infinite.

派生· transformation *n.* 转换；变形

搭配· 使某物 / 某人转变成…… transform sth./sb. into sth.

hinder ['hɪndər]

释义· *v.* 阻碍；妨碍；阻挡

例句· 在某些情况下，现有的技术甚至可能阻碍团队协作和服务建议的快速转变。

In some cases, existing technology may even hinder team collaboration and rapid turnaround of service proposals.

派生· hindrance *n.* 阻碍；妨碍；障碍物

搭配· 阻碍某人 / 某物做某事 hinder sb./sth. from doing sth.

mechanically [mə'kænɪkli]

释义 · *adj.* 机械地；呆板地

例句 · 这辆车的零部件没有问题，他判定道。

The car was mechanically sound, he decided.

patent ['pætnt]

释义 · *vt.* 获得专利权 *n.* 专利权；专利证书 *adj.* 有专利的；明显的

例句 · 那项发明已被那所大学申请了专利。

The invention has been patented by the university.

搭配 · 国家专利 national patent

authentic [ɔː'θentɪk]

释义 · *adj.* 真正的；真实的；可信的

例句 · 对人类和环境的真正的担忧需要研究、准确性和真正的科学怀疑主义。

Genuine concern for humankind and the environment demands the inquiry, accuracy and skepticism of authentic science.

派生 · authenticate *vt.* 鉴定；证明……是真实的

authenticity *n.* 真实性；确实性

forecast ['fɔːrkæst]

释义 · *v.* 预测；预报 *n.* 预测；预报

例句 · 科学家们预测，在未来的十年里，材料科学将取得突破。

Scientists forecast that there will be breakthroughs in material science in the next decade.

派生 · forecaster *n.* 预报员

搭配 · 天气预报 weather forecast

扩展 · forecast/forecasted（过去式）forecast/forecasted（过去分词）

conceivable [kən'si:vəbl]

释义· *adj.* 可想象的；可信的

例句· 可以想象，诺基亚（NOK）在整合类似技术方面可能紧随三星之后。

It is conceivable that Nokia (NOK) may be close behind Samsung in incorporating similar technology.

transition [træn'zɪʃn]

释义· *n.* 转变；过渡；变迁 *v.*（从某一状态或活动）转变

例句· 从模拟电视到数字电视的转变花了 50 多年的时间。

It took more than 50 sleepy years to begin the transition from analogue television to digital.

派生· transitional *adj.*（时期）过渡的；过渡性的

搭配· 从……过渡到…… transition from sth. to sth.

omnipotent [ɑ:m'nɪpətənt]

释义· *adj.* 无所不能的；全能的

例句· 计算机的工作就是通过计算机的软件组，充分利用计算机的各种资源，并指挥硬件实现无所不能的奇妙用途。

The work of a computer is just making full use of various resources by software set in the computer, and directing the hardware to realize marvelous omnipotent functions.

派生· omnipotence *n.* 全能；无限权力；无所不能

atmosphere ['ætməsfɪr]

释义· *n.* 大气；气氛

例句· 有可靠的科学依据可以证明某些气体对大气的影响。

There is sound scientific evidence of what certain gases do to the atmosphere.

symbol ['sɪmbl]

释义· *n.* 象征；符号；标志

例句· 蒸汽机是第一次工业革命的象征。

The steam engine was the symbol of the first industrial revolution.

派生· symbolic *adj.* 象征性的

symbolize *v.* 象征；是……的象征

depletion [dɪ'pliːʃn]

释义· *n.* (U) 消耗；损耗

例句· 过度捕捞不仅引起个别鱼种的消耗，而且还引起海洋中整个生态系统和食物网的崩溃。

Overfishing not only causes depletion in individual fish stocks, but also disruption to entire ecosystems and food webs in the ocean.

同根· depleted *adj.* 耗尽的；废弃的

accomplish [ə'kɑːmplɪʃ]

释义· *vt.* 完成；达成

例句· 为了完成这两项任务，我们需要向科学技术和人力资源注入资金。

To accomplish both tasks, we need to pump money into scientific technology and human resource.

派生· accomplished *adj.* 熟练的；才华高的；有造诣的

accomplishment *n.* 成就；完成；技艺

搭配· 一事无成 accomplish nothing

alarm [ə'lɑːrm]

释义· *n.* 惊慌；警报；闹钟 *vt.* 使惊恐；使害怕

例句· 对于近期的火山爆发，科学家们说不必惊慌。

For the recent eruption of the volcano, scientists have said there is no cause for alarm.

派生· alarming *adj.* 令人担忧的；使人惊恐的
搭配· 惊慌；在惊恐中 in alarm

nearsighted [ˌnɪr'saɪtɪd]

释义· *adj.* 目光短浅的；近视的
例句· 事实证明，那些批评霍金新理论的人是目光短浅的。
Facts can prove that those who criticize Hawking's new theory at the beginning are nearsighted.
反义· far-sighted *adj.* 有远见的；深谋远虑的
派生· nearsightedness *n.* 目光短浅；近视眼

achievement [ə'tʃiːvmənt]

释义· *n.* 成就；成绩；完成
例句· 这项科研非常复杂，如果开发者能做到，这将是一个伟大的成就。
This scientific research is very complicated, so if developers can do this, it would be a massive achievement.
同根· achievable *adj.* 可达到的；可获得的
搭配· 学业成绩 academic achievement

exploit [ɪk'splɔɪt]

释义· *vt.* 利用；开发；开采；剥削
例句· 如果我们要充分利用这种新技术，我们需要同时考虑这两者。
We have to consider both if we are to exploit this new technology to its full extent.
派生· exploiter *n.* 剥削者；压榨者

manual ['mænjuəl]

释义· *adj.* 体力的；手工的 *n.* 使用手册；指南

例句· 机器代替了体力劳动，使我们有了更多的闲暇时间，也使得一部分人失业了。

Machine replaces the manual labor, which brings us more leisure time and causes some people unemployment as well.

派生· manually *adv.* 手动地

搭配· 处于非自动状态；处于手动状态 on manual

undermine [ˌʌndər'maɪn]

释义· *vt.* 逐渐损害；渐渐破坏

例句· 手机辐射可能会损害使用者的健康，所以睡觉时请远离手机。

The radiation of a cell phone may undermine the health of the user, so stay away from your phone while you sleep.

distinguish [dɪ'stɪŋgwɪʃ]

释义· *v.* 区别；辨别；使有别于

例句· 我们可以根据物质的特性把一种物质与另一种物质辨别开来。

We can distinguish one kind of substance from another by its properties.

派生· distinguishable *adj.* 可以区别开的；可辨认的

搭配· 把 A 和 B 区分开来 distinguish A from B

（作为……）某人享有盛名 distinguish yourself (as sth.)

adopt [ə'dɑːpt]

释义· *v.* 采取；采纳；收养

例句· 这并不是为了限制社会研究人员所能采用的方法。

This is not meant to delimit what approaches social researchers can adopt.

派生· adoption *n.* 采用；收养

adoptive *adj.* 收养的；有收养关系的

adopted *adj.* 收养的；领养的

搭配· 采用某种方法 / 态度 adopt an approach/attitude

sedentary ['sednteri]

释义· *adj.* 需要久坐的；长期伏案的；定居的

例句· 科技让我们适应了久坐不动的生活，这不利于我们的健康。

Technology has made us adapt to a sedentary life, which has a bad influence on our health.

搭配· sedentary lifestyle 长期久坐的生活方式

device [dɪ'vaɪs]

释义· *n.* 设备；仪器；方法；手段

例句· 这个设备驱动程序需要对设备本身执行一些诊断操作。

This device driver should perform some diagnostics of the device itself.

搭配· 做某事的方法 a device for doing sth.

electronic [ɪˌlek'trɑːnɪk]

释义· *adj.* 电子的；电子化的

例句· 电子计算机在科学技术方面广泛的应用将使人们从复杂的计量和计算中摆脱出来。

The wide application of electronic computers in science and technology will free man from the labor of complicated measurement and computation.

同根· electronics *n.* 电子学

搭配· 电子游戏 electronic games

电网 electricity grid

ingenious [ɪn'dʒiːniəs]

释义· *adj.* 机敏的；心灵手巧的；善于创造发明的

例句· 聪明的科学家和工程师创造了一些相当令人惊讶的精巧小玩意儿。

Ingenious scientists and engineers have created some pretty amazing gadgets.

派生· ingeniousness *n.* 机敏；聪明

anticipate [æn'tɪsɪpeɪt]

释义· *v.* 预料；预期；先于……做

例句· 那时我们不可能预料到我们这项科学研究的结果。

At the time we couldn't have anticipated the result of our scientific research.

派生· anticipation *n.* 预料；期盼

anticipatory *adj.* 期待的；期望的

搭配· 预期 / 预料做某事　anticipate doing sth.

细心考虑　anticipate over

proliferation [prə,lɪfə'reɪʃn]

释义· *n.* (U) 激增；增殖；扩散

例句· 全球媒体网络的激增对我们的隐私构成了威胁。

The proliferation of global media networks pose a threat to our privacy.

搭配· 核扩散　nuclear proliferation

labor ['leɪbər]

释义· *n.* 劳动；（尤指）体力劳动；分娩 *v.* 劳动；艰苦地做

例句· 如果将这些机器应用于农业，将会为农民节省大量劳动。

If they are applied in agriculture, the machines will save farmers much labor.

搭配· 劳动力　labor force

劳动力的分工 division of labor

conscience ['kɑ:nʃəns]

释义· *n.* 良知；良心

例句· 克隆人的问题一直折磨着人类的良知。

The question of human cloning has been torturing the conscience of humanity.

派生· conscientious *adj.* 勤勉认真的；一丝不苟的

搭配· 对（某事）不愧疚 have no conscience (about sth.)

使人内疚；良心不安 on your conscience

boon [bu:n]

释义· *n.* 非常有用的东西；益处

例句· 科学是把双刃剑，给人类带来恩惠的同时也可能带来灾难。

Science, a double-edged sword, not only can bring boon but a disaster for humankind.

transaction [træn'zækʃn]

释义· *n.* （一笔）业务，交易，买卖

例句· 通过网络金融业务，人们可以随时随地管理自己的资产。

Through the network financial transaction, people can manage their assets anytime and anywhere.

搭配· 现金交易 cash transaction

商业交易 commercial transaction

manned [mænd]

释义· *adj.* 载人的；由人操纵的

例句· 未来 30 年内，美国有可能会把载人航天器送上火星。

In thirty years from now the United States should have a manned spacecraft on Mars.

反义· unmanned *adj.* 无人驾驶的

progress ['prɑːgres]

释义· *n.* (U) 进步；前进
例句· 21 世纪的科技进步将改变人类社会。
The technological progress of the twenty-first century will change human society.
派生· progressive *adj.* 进步的；先进的
搭配· 取得进步 make/achieve progress
在进行中 in progress

efficiency [ɪ'fɪʃnsi]

释义· *n.* 效率；效能
例句· 公司引进的新技术提高了效率。
New technology introduced by the company has brought efficiency gains.
搭配· 效率的提高 improvements in efficiency

standardize ['stændərdaɪz]

释义· *vt.* 使标准化；使符合标准（或规格）
例句· 正在为实现零部件标准化和减少推出的型号数量而努力。
There is a drive both to standardize components and to reduce the number of models on offer.
派生· standardization *n.* 标准化
搭配· 标准化合同 / 设计 / 考试 a standardized contract/design/test

empower [ɪm'paʊər]

释义· *vt.* 授权；给予……权力
例句· 我们的任务是对 IT 架构的专业化进行发展、规范和授权。
Our mission is to develop, formalize and empower the

profession of IT architecture.

派生· empowerment *n.* 授权

universal [ˌjuːnɪˈvɜːrsl]

释义· *adj.* 普遍存在的；广泛适用的；宇宙的

例句· 万有引力的发现是 17 世纪自然科学最伟大的成就之一。

The discovery of universal gravitation is one of the greatest achievements of natural science in the 17th century.

派生· universality *n.* 普遍性；广泛性

stride [straɪd]

释义· *n.* 进步；发展 *v.* 阔步行走；大步走

例句· 这个国家在科学方面取得了巨大进步，包括将一颗卫星发射到火星的轨道上。

The country has made enormous strides in science, including launching a satellite into the orbit of Mars.

搭配· 从容处理；泰然处之 take sth. in stride

开始顺利地做某事 get into one's stride

尽量不落后（于某人）(match sb.) stride for stride

escalate [ˈeskəleɪt]

释义· *v.* （使）逐步扩大，不断恶化，加剧

例句· 我们必须采用最新的技术，淘汰旧技术，否则成本将急剧上升。

We must adopt the latest technology and eliminate the old; otherwise, the costs will escalate alarmingly.

搭配· 逐步扩大为 escalate into

optimize [ˈɑːptɪmaɪz]

释义· *v.* 使最优化；充分利用

例句· 要优化应用程序的性能，就应该尝试最小化每个组件的等待

时间。

To optimize the performance of an application, you should attempt to minimize the wait time for each component.

同根· optimization *n.* 最优化

encyclopedia [ɪnˌsaɪkləˈpiːdiə]

释义· *n.* 百科全书

例句· 全球教科书项目在技术上类似于维基百科，这是一种任何人都可以在互联网上编辑的免费百科全书。

The Global Text Project is similar in technology to Wikipedia, the free encyclopedia that anyone can edit on the Internet.

deprive [dɪˈpraɪv]

释义· *v.* 剥夺；使丧失

例句· 在某种意义上，电子产品剥夺了我们的自由。

In a sense, electronic products deprive us of our freedom.

派生· deprived *adj.* 贫困的；穷苦的

搭配· 剥夺某人某物 deprive sb. of sth.

systematic [ˌsɪstəˈmætɪk]

释义· *adj.* 系统的；有条理的；有计划的

例句· 软件方法是关于如何开发软件的系统性方法和控制。

A software methodology is a systematic approach and control of how to develop software.

派生· systematically *adv.* 系统地；有组织地

释义	短语
最新技术	latest technology/cutting-edge technology
对……产生深远的影响	exert a far-reaching impact on
双刃剑	double-edged sword
踏上；登上	set foot on
过多的选择	plethora of choices
担忧……	be concerned about
对……造成威胁	pose a threat to
虚假信息	fake and exaggerated information
网上购物	shopping online
电子商务	e-business
基因工程	genetic engineering
引起关注	raise concerns
目光短浅的	short-sighted
冒……的风险	run the risk of
对……视而不见	turn a blind eye to
对……置若罔闻	turn a deaf ear to
支柱产业	a pillar industry

突飞猛进	advance by/improve in leaps and bounds
尖端设备	sophisticated equipment
信息时代	the information age
平板电脑	tablet computer
映入我们的眼帘	jump into our sight
因特网时代	the era/age of Internet
自动驾驶汽车	autonomous vehicles
社交网站	social networking site
在各行各业	in all walks of life
融入我们的日常生活	embedded in our daily lives
便于使用的	user-friendly
打车软件	ride-hailing app
知识产权	intellectual property
使人成为技术的奴隶	render people slaves to technology
盗版软件	pirated software
星际空间	interstellar space
处在……的边缘	be on the verge of

托福写作场景词汇

巩固练习

练习1 根据下面的中文释义，写出对应的单词（词组）。

A

普遍存在的 u＿＿＿＿

业务 t＿＿＿＿

先进的 a＿＿＿＿

更新 u＿＿＿＿

逐渐损害 u＿＿＿＿

打车软件 r＿＿＿＿

最新技术 l＿＿＿＿

利用 e＿＿＿＿

体力的 m＿＿＿＿

模拟 s＿＿＿＿

天堂 p＿＿＿＿

B

在各行各业 i＿＿＿＿

激增 p＿＿＿＿

预料 a＿＿＿＿

（能源）替代的 a＿＿＿＿

幻想 f＿＿＿＿

机敏的 i＿＿＿＿

新奇的 n＿＿＿＿

设备 a＿＿＿＿

前所未有的 u＿＿＿＿

给……蒙上阴影 o＿＿＿＿

抑制 c＿＿＿＿

练习2 用方框中所给单词（词组）的适当形式填空。

utilize	surpass	substitute for	terminate
compute	mitigate	converge	track down
symbol	breakthrough	deprive	transform into
conscience	accomplish	redundant	

1. Sound engineers u＿＿＿＿（运用）a range of techniques to enhance the quality of the recordings.

262

2. Some scientists are worried about that AI will s_____ (超过) the IQ of the human being in the future.

3. This APP can t_____ (查到) the users' data to better serve the clients.

4. Changes in technology may mean that once-valued skills are now r_____ (多余的).

5. Computers can c_____ (计算) this complex equation within seconds.

6. Natural gas, clean and cheap, is a good s_____ (替代) coal.

7. Measures need to be taken to m_____ (减轻) the environmental effects of burning more coal.

8. Scientists have made a b_____ (突破) in the treatment of cancer.

9. Someone says that the human history will be t_____ (结束) by artificial intelligence.

10. This machine c_____ (汇聚) the latest OS and scientific payoffs and the most fashionable design.

11. Wind, water and sun can be t_____ (转化为) electricity, and these resources are infinite.

12. The steam engine was the s_____ (象征) of the first industrial revolution.

13. To a_____ (完成) both tasks, we need to pump money into scientific technology and human resource.

14. The question of human cloning has been torturing the c_____ (良知) of humanity.

15. In a sense, electronic products d_____ (剥夺) us of our freedom.

☐ advanced	☐ apparatus	☐ launch
☐ dimension	☐ redundant	☐ mitigate
☐ abundance	☐ replicate	☐ perpetual
☐ utilize	☐ span	☐ soar
☐ scientific	☐ invent	☐ explosion
☐ display	☐ accelerate	☐ staggering
☐ dramatic	☐ transportation	☐ cozy
☐ functional	☐ artificial	☐ breakthrough
☐ cyber	☐ compute	☐ virtual
☐ milestone	☐ mass	☐ investigate
☐ surpass	☐ alternative	☐ terminate
☐ antibiotics	☐ exploration	☐ global
☐ antithetical	☐ fantasy	☐ revolution
☐ commercialized	☐ convey	☐ dominant
☐ vehicle	☐ automatic	☐ novel
☐ malicious	☐ substitute	☐ renewable
☐ deterioration	☐ innovation	☐ extinction
☐ overcrowded	☐ derive	☐ probe
☐ gravity	☐ infinite	☐ update
☐ track	☐ unprecedented	☐ supersede
☐ boundary	☐ static	☐ assemble
☐ overshadow	☐ operation	☐ paradise
☐ hazard	☐ dense	☐ productive
☐ curb	☐ appliance	☐ converge

☐ hack	☐ alarm	☐ conscience
☐ simulate	☐ nearsighted	☐ boon
☐ transform	☐ achievement	☐ transaction
☐ hinder	☐ exploit	☐ manned
☐ mechanically	☐ manual	☐ progress
☐ patent	☐ undermine	☐ efficiency
☐ authentic	☐ distinguish	☐ standardize
☐ forecast	☐ adopt	☐ empower
☐ conceivable	☐ sedentary	☐ universal
☐ transition	☐ device	☐ stride
☐ omnipotent	☐ electronic	☐ escalate
☐ atmosphere	☐ ingenious	☐ optimize
☐ symbol	☐ anticipate	☐ encyclopedia
☐ depletion	☐ proliferation	☐ deprive
☐ accomplish	☐ labor	☐ systematic

表中共有 117 个单词

您不确认的单词 _____ 个，占总数的 _____%

如果比例高于 10%，请耐心再复习一遍。如果比例低于 10%，您可以开始下一章的托福写作之旅了！

第八章

媒体

fabricate ['fæbrɪkeɪt]

释义· *vt.* 捏造；编造；制造

例句· 新闻工作者不应该捏造新闻，也不应该抄袭剽窃，即抄用他人文章而不注明出处。

Journalists should not fabricate news, nor should they plagiarize—that is, copy without attribution—another person's work.

搭配· 制造谣言 fabricate rumors

捏造证据 fabricate evidence

affair [ə'fer]

释义· *n.* 事务；事件

例句· 我不准备和媒体讨论我的财务问题。

I am not prepared to discuss my financial affairs with the press.

搭配· 某人的私事 sb.'s private affairs

时事　current affairs

国务　affairs of state

paparazzi [ˌpæpəˈrætsi]

释义· *n.* (*pl.*) 狗仔队

例句· 阿玛尼走到哪儿，狗仔队就跟到哪儿。

The paparazzi pursue Armani wherever he travels.

扩展· paparazzo (*sing.*)

celebrity [səˈlebrəti]

释义· *n.* 名人；名望

例句· 他不仅仅是足球场上的巨星，也是一位社会名流。

He was more than a footballing superstar; he was a celebrity.

搭配· 明星效应；名人效应　celebrity effect

追星族　celebrity worshipper

名人代言　celebrity endorsement

sitcom [ˈsɪtkɑːm]

释义· *n.* 情景喜剧

例句· 38 岁的安妮斯顿凭借情景喜剧《老友记》走红。2005 年，她与皮特结束了维持四年半的婚姻。

Former star of TV sitcom *Friends*, Anniston, 38, and Pitt got divorced in 2005 after four-and-a-half years of marriage.

censorship [ˈsensərʃɪp]

释义· *n.* (U) 审查制度；审查；检查

例句· 政府今天宣布将取消新闻审查制度。

The government today announced that press censorship was being lifted.

sway [sweɪ]

释义· *n.* (U) 影响；摇摆；统治 *v.*（使）摇摆；说服

例句· 他是怎么在公众中获得如此大的影响力，以至于大家都开始不信任当权的政府和正统的媒体？

How did he come to hold such sway with a public that had begun to distrust both the establishment government and the establishment media?

搭配· 在某人的控制下 under one's sway

distort [dɪ'stɔ:rt]

释义· *vt.* 歪曲；曲解；使变形

例句· 媒体会歪曲事实，将人说得不是完美无缺就是一无是处。

The media distorts reality; it categorizes people as all good or all bad.

派生· distorted *adj.* 歪曲的；受到曲解的

distortion *n.* 变形；曲解；失真

fraudulent ['frɔ:dʒələnt]

释义· *adj.* 欺骗性的；欺诈性的

例句· 广告中的一些内容是虚假的。

Some of the content in the advertisement is fraudulent.

派生· fraudulence *n.* 欺诈；欺骗性

expose [ɪk'spoʊz]

释义· *vt.* 揭露；揭发；使暴露

例句· 这是一篇关于新闻界如何协助揭露尼克松政府真相的报道。

It is a story of how the press helped expose the truth about the Nixon administration.

派生· exposed *adj.* 无掩蔽的

exposure *n.* 暴露；曝光；揭露

搭配· 使某人接触某物 expose sb. to sth.

widespread ['waɪdspred]

释义· *adj.* 广泛的；普遍的；分布广的

例句· 这则新闻在世界各地广为流传。

This news is widespread all over the world.

同义· universal *adj.* 普遍的；全体的；全世界的

搭配· 广泛用于…… widespread use in

subscribe [səb'skraɪb]

释义· *v.* 订阅，订购（杂志或报纸）；定期捐款；认购（股份）

例句· 我订阅《新科学家》主要是为了了解科学的最新进展。

My main reason for subscribing to *New Scientist* is to keep abreast of advances in science.

派生· subscription *n.* 订阅费；会员费；用户费

搭配· 同意 / 赞成某事 subscribe to sth.

fame [feɪm]

释义· *n.* (U) 名声；名望；声誉

例句· 这件丑闻将无损于她的名声。

The scandal will not detract from her fame.

搭配· 一夜成名 rise/shoot to fame overnight

一举成名 shoot to fame

名与利 fame and fortune

名人堂 hall of fame

虚誉；虚名 empty fame

popularity [ˌpɑːpjuˈlærəti]

释义· *n.* (U) 流行；普及；受欢迎

例句· 尽管网络在 50 岁以上的人群中颇为流行，报纸和杂志仍是他们首选的消息来源。

Despite the popularity of the Internet among the over 50s, print newspapers and magazines are still their preferred source for news.

同根· popularize *v.* 使受欢迎；推广；使通俗；普及

搭配· 享有盛誉 enjoy great popularity

开始流行 gain/grow/increase in popularity

issue ['ɪʃuː]

释义· *n.* （报刊的）期；重要问题 *v.* 发布；发表

例句· 最新一期的《科学美国人》杂志中强调了这一日益严重的问题。

The growing problem is underlined in the latest issue of the *Scientific American*.

搭配· 是讨论的焦点 be at issue

（就某事）向某人提出异议 take issue with sb. (about/on/over sth.)

对（某人／某事）有异议 have issues (with sb./sth.)

从……中出来 issue from sth.

newsworthy ['nuːzwɜːrði]

释义· *adj.* 有新闻价值的；值得报道的

例句· 后继报道往往会带来比即时报道更有新闻价值的惊人进展。

Follow-ups often lead to surprising developments that are even more newsworthy than the original report.

coverage ['kʌvərɪdʒ]

释义· *n.* 新闻报道；采访

例句· 现在有一个专门的电视网络对大部分比赛进行现场直播。

Now a special TV network gives live coverage of most races.

搭配· 媒体 / 报纸 / 报刊的报道 media/newspaper/press coverage

journal ['dʒɜːrnl]

释义· n.（某学科或专业的）杂志，报纸，刊物；日记；日志

例句· 这项研究将于明天发表在美国《科学》杂志上。

The research will be published in the US journal *Science* tomorrow.

派生· journalist n. 新闻工作者

journalism n. 新闻业；新闻工作

搭配· 学术期刊 academic journal

日报 daily journal

spotlight ['spɑːtlaɪt]

释义· n. 媒体和公众的注意；聚光灯 vt. 使突出醒目；使受关注

例句· 一篇新的报道使人们将关注的目光投向市中心贫民区的贫困问题。

A new report has turned the spotlight on the problem of poverty in the inner cities.

搭配· 在关注下；成为焦点 in/under the spotlight

某事成为人们关注的焦点 put/turn the spotlight on sth.

propaganda [ˌprɑːpəˈgændə]

释义· n. (U) 宣传；鼓吹（含贬义）

例句· 这家报社是政府的宣传机器。

This newspaper office is the government propaganda machine.

搭配· 系列宣传活动 a propaganda campaign

network ['netwɜːrk]

释义· n. 广播网；电视网；网络；网状系统 v. 建立工作关系网

例句· 位于洛杉矶的"联合视野"是一家西班牙语的广播电视网。

Los Angeles-based Univision is a Spanish-language broadcast television network.

搭配· 校友关系网 the old boy network

press [pres]

释义· *n.* 报纸；报刊；新闻；出版社 *v.* 压；按；极力要求

例句· 此事在全国性报纸上广为报道。

The story was widely covered in the national press.

搭配· 新闻发布 press release

记者招待会；新闻发布会 press conference

正在印刷；即将出版 go to press

新闻界 the press

witness ['wɪtnəs]

释义· *v.* 目击；见证 *n.* 证人；目击者

例句· 很少有人会让媒体目击他们在做什么，因为隐私是他们最看重的。

Few will let the media in to witness what they do because privacy is the most critical issue they value.

搭配· 目击 / 看见某事发生 be (a) witness to sth.

subtitle ['sʌbtaɪtl]

释义· *n.* 副标题；小标题 *v.* 给……加副标题

例句· 打造和传播此类品牌是我在书的副标题中声称"中国消费主义将改变一切"的一个原因。

The creation and spread of such brands is one reason I claim in the subtitle of my book that Chinese consumerism will change "everything."

edit ['edɪt]

释义· v. 校订；编辑；编选 n. 编辑；校订

例句· 这家报社刊登读者来信前先作校订。

The newspaper edits letters before printing them.

派生· editor n. 编辑；编者

editorial adj. 编辑的；主编的 n. 社论

privacy ['praɪvəsi]

释义· n. (U) 隐私；私密；独处

例句· 你应该调整在网站上的隐私设置，以确保你的个人详细资料或照片只能让你所选定的人看到。

You should adjust your privacy settings on the Web to ensure personal details or photos are available only to the people you select.

搭配· 隐私权　the right to privacy

个人隐私　individual privacy

侵犯个人隐私　invasion of privacy

violate ['vaɪəleɪt]

释义· vt. 侵犯（隐私）；违反（协议等）

例句· 媒体经常会侵犯人们的隐私。

The media regularly violates people's privacy.

派生· violation n. 违反；妨碍

搭配· 触犯法律；违法　violate the law

objective [əb'dʒektɪv]

释义· adj. 客观的；不带个人感情的 n. 目的；目标

例句· 每个人都应该认识到一个完全客观、独立的新闻媒体的重要性。

Everyone should realize the importance of a completely

objective, independent press.

反义· subjective *adj.* 主观的

派生· objectivity *n.* 客观性

headline ['hedlaɪn]

释义· *n.* （报纸的）大字标题 *vt.* 给（报道、文章）加标题

例句· 这家报纸把那条消息以大字标题宣扬出去。

The news was blazed in headline of the newspaper.

搭配· 成为重要新闻 make/grab/hit the headlines

publication [ˌpʌblɪˈkeɪʃn]

释义· *n.* 出版物；出版

例句· 你正在免费读这篇文章，但这个出版物通过在你看的页面上卖广告赚钱。

You're reading this for free, but the publication makes money by selling the advertising you see on this page.

搭配· 出版日期 the publication date

专业出版物 specialist publications

scandal ['skændl]

释义· *n.* 丑闻；流言蜚语；令人气愤的事

例句· 这本杂志登载的全是八卦内容。

The magazine is full of gossip and scandal.

派生· scandalous *adj.* 讲述丑闻的

scandalize *vt.* 使震惊；使愤慨

搭配· 令人震惊；不能接受 be a scandal

relevance ['reləvəns]

释义· *n.* (U) 相关性；（对……的）重要性；意义

例句· 不断被来自媒体的不确定的关联信息狂轰乱炸，人们会变得困惑，

很难做出决定。

Bombarded constantly by information of dubious relevance from media, people would become confused and struggle to make decisions.

overrate [ˌoʊvərˈreɪt]

释义· v. 高估；对……评价过高

例句· 依我看赫斯特的作品被大大地高估了。

In my opinion, Hirst's work has been vastly overrated.

反义· underrate vt. 过低评价；低估

flyer [ˈflaɪər]

释义· n. （广告）宣传单；飞行员；飞机乘客

例句· 节日期间散发了数千份推广这项旅游的宣传单。

Thousands of flyers advertising the tour were handed out during the festival.

addiction [əˈdɪkʃn]

释义· n. 瘾；入迷；嗜好

例句· 媒体应该宣传网络成瘾的危害。

The media should publicize the dangers of Internet addiction.

misleading [ˌmɪsˈliːdɪŋ]

释义· adj. 使人产生误解的；误导人的

例句· 这篇文章具有误导性，那家报纸已经道歉了。

The article was misleading, and the newspaper has apologized.

搭配· 使人产生误解的信息 / 广告 misleading information/advertisements

误导行为 misleading behavior

icon ['aɪkɑːn]

释义· *n.* 偶像；代表人物；图标

例句· 如今，各种娱乐节目产生了许多时尚偶像。
Various entertainment programs produced many fashion icons today.

派生· iconic *adj.* 偶像的；图符的
iconoclastic *adj.* 有悖传统信仰的

搭配· 女权主义者的偶像 a feminist icon

informative [ɪn'fɔːrmətɪv]

释义· *adj.* 提供有用消息（或资料）的；增长知识的

例句· 这些广告并没有包含太多有用信息。
The adverts are not very informative.

plot [plɑːt]

释义· *n.* 故事情节；阴谋 *v.* 密谋；绘制（图表）；计划

例句· 这部小说的情节就如同宣传的那样错综复杂，引人入胜。
The plot of the novel, as advertised, is intricate and fascinating.

搭配· 与 A 密谋推翻 B plot with A against B

disguise [dɪs'gaɪz]

释义· *vt.* 掩饰；假装；假扮 *n.* 伪装；伪装物

例句· 她利用大量的新闻报道来掩饰自己不光彩的历史。
She used a lot of news coverage to disguise her shameful history.

搭配· 把自己伪装成某人 / 某物 disguise yourself as sb./sth.
乔装；伪装 in disguise
因祸得福；祸中有福 a blessing in disguise

sensational [sen'seɪʃənl]

释义· *adj.* 耸人听闻的；哗众取宠的；轰动的；极好的

例句· 这类报纸满是耸人听闻的新闻报道。

Papers of this kind are full of sensational news reports.

派生· sensationally *adv.* 耸人听闻地

rating ['reɪtɪŋ]

释义· *n.* （电视节目的）收视率；评级；电影的等级

例句· 与前一年相比，哥伦比亚广播公司的收视率再次大幅提高。

CBS's ratings again showed huge improvement over the previous year.

imperative [ɪm'perətɪv]

释义· *adj.* 必要的；紧急的；表示权威的 *n.* 必要的事

例句· 净化低俗广告是必要的。

Purifying vulgar advertisements is imperative.

medium ['mi:diəm]

释义· *n.* （传播信息的）媒介，手段，方法 *adj.* 中等的

例句· 广告是一种强有力的传播媒介。

Advertising is a powerful medium.

扩展· media/mediums (*pl.*)

impressionable [ɪm'preʃənəbl]

释义· *adj.* （通常指年轻人）易受影响的，无主见的，无判断力的

例句· 该法律意图保护那些年轻且无判断力的电视观众，因为有些电影有血腥或暴力的场景。

The law is intended to protect young and impressionable viewers because some movies have bloody or violent scenes.

vulgarity [vʌl'gærəti]

释义· *n.* 庸俗；粗俗

例句· 但也有一些批评者形容该节目是"披着自救外衣的庸俗行为"。

However, some critics have described the program as "vulgarity disguised as self-help."

premiere [prɪ'mɪr]

释义· *n.* 首映；初次公演

例句· 自 1977 年首映以来,《星球大战》几乎渗入到每一种亚文化之中, 蒸汽朋克也不例外。

Star Wars has leaked into nearly every subculture since its premiere in 1977, and steampunk is no exception.

theme [θiːm]

释义· *n.* (演讲、文章或艺术作品的)主题,题目,主题思想

例句· 随着女权主义的传播和推广,现在好莱坞电影的主题是女性。

With the spread and promotion of feminism, now the central theme of Hollywood movies are women.

派生· thematic *adj.* 主题的；专题的；题目的

搭配· 主题公园 theme park

indecent [ɪn'diːsnt]

释义· *adj.* 下流的；不合时宜的

例句· 所有媒体不得发布、张贴、分发或散布任何诽谤、侵权、淫秽、下流或非法的材料或信息。

All media cannot publish, post, distribute or disseminate any defamatory, infringing, obscene, indecent or unlawful material or information.

反义· decent *adj.* 正派的；得体的；相当不错的

flowery ['flaʊəri]

释义· *adj.*（演说或文章）词藻华丽的

例句· 这家报纸使用了极其华丽的词藻，但内容空洞。

This newspaper was using uncommonly flowery language, but the content is empty.

bestseller [ˌbest'selər]

释义· *n.* 畅销书

例句· 这些书被翻译成 27 种文字，并登上了好几个国家的畅销书排行榜。

The books have been translated into 27 languages and appeared on bestseller charts in several of those countries.

同义· big hits 大卖商品；畅销商品；（电影、戏剧等）大受欢迎

audience ['ɔːdiəns]

释义· *n.* 观众；听众

例句· 这个节目吸引了大约两千万固定观众收看。

The show attracts a regular audience of about 20 million.

搭配· 目标受众；目标观众 target audience

收视率；视听率 audience rating

poster ['poʊstər]

释义· *n.* 海报；大幅广告；招贴画

例句· 每幅海报都有这个艺术家的签名。

Each poster is signed by the artist.

搭配· 典型人物 poster child

commercialized [kə'mɜːrʃəlaɪzd]

释义· *adj.* 商业化的

例句· 这个电视节目的推广也日渐商业化了。

Also the promotion of this TV show is getting too commercialized now.

同根· commercial *adj.* 商业的 *n.* 商业广告

billboard ['bɪlbɔːrd]

释义· *n.* 广告牌；布告栏

例句· 站台上的一幅巨幅广告牌吸引了她的注意力。

An advertising billboard on the platform caught her attention.

delete [dɪ'liːt]

释义· *vt.* 删除；删去

例句· 政府要求各家报纸删除有关腐败的报道。

The government has asked newspapers to delete stories about corruption.

reveal [rɪ'viːl]

释义· *v.* 透露；揭示；显示

例句· 地方报纸披露了谋杀的细节。

Details of the murder were revealed by the local paper.

同义· disclose *v.* 揭露；透露；泄露

派生· revealing *adj.* 透露真相的；发人深省的；暴露的

groupie ['gruːpi]

释义· *n.* 粉丝（尤指少女）

例句· 我向他直言，说他只不过是个政治上的狂热追随者。

I put it to him that he was just a political groupie.

whitewash ['waɪtwɑːʃ]

释义· *v.* 粉饰；掩饰 *n.* 粉饰

例句· 政府正在粉饰该政权的行为，但媒体正在揭露事实。

The administration is whitewashing the regime's actions, but the media is exposing the truth.

hype [haɪp]

释义· *n.* (U) 炒作；大肆宣传 *vt.* 大肆宣传；炒作

例句· 尽管媒体大肆炒作，我还是觉得这部影片很让人失望。

Despite the media hype, I found the film very disappointing.

搭配· 夸张的促销 / 媒体广告　marketing/media hype

mainstream ['meɪnstriːm]

释义· *adj.* 主流的 *n.* （人、活动等的）主流 *v.* 使为大多数人所接受

例句· 现在的父母需要担心的是性、毒品和互联网，或者至少是那些主流媒体中传播的有害的网站信息。

Now parents have to worry about sex, drugs and the Internet—or at least the bad and evil Internet as propagated by the mainstream media.

搭配· 主流媒体　mainstream media

主流文化　mainstream culture

episode ['epɪsoʊd]

释义· *n.* （电视剧的）一集；（小说的）一节；插曲

例句· 最后一集将于下周日播放。

The final episode will be shown next Sunday.

saturate ['sætʃəreɪt]

释义· *vt.* 使充满；使饱和；浸透

例句· 我们的文化里充斥着电视和广告。

Our culture is saturated with television and advertising.

派生· saturated *adj.* 饱和的

saturation *n.* 饱和；饱和状态

digital ['dɪdʒɪtl]

释义· *adj.* 数码的；数字的

例句· 新的数字技术将会使电视频道的数量迅速增加。

The new digital technology would allow a rapid expansion in the number of TV channels.

搭配· 数字图书馆 digital library

数字媒体；数码媒体 digital media

anecdote ['ænɪkdoʊt]

释义· *n.* 逸事；趣闻；传闻

例句· 报纸上全是超级明星们生活的趣闻逸事。

The newspaper is full of amusing anecdotes about superstars' life.

派生· anecdotal *adj.* 逸事的，趣闻的

搭配· 个人逸事 personal anecdote

splash [splæʃ]

释义· *v.* （报刊）以醒目方式刊登；飞溅 *n.* 落水声；溅上的液体

例句· 持枪歹徒的照片刊登在了报纸头版显著位置。

The gunman's picture was splashed across the front page of the newspaper.

搭配· 花大笔的钱（买某物）splash out (on sth.)

引起广泛关注；引起轰动 make/cause a splash

brainwash ['breɪnwɔːʃ]

释义· *v.* 给……洗脑；向……强行灌输

例句· 商业广告促使消费者去买那些他们不需要的东西。

Commercials brainwash consumers into buying things they don't need.

派生· brainwashing *n.* 洗脑

搭配· 给某人洗脑以做某事　brainwash sb. into doing sth.

cogent ['koʊdʒənt]

释义· *adj.* 令人信服的；有说服力的

例句· 每一篇新闻报道都必须有合理和令人信服的论据做支持。

Each news report has to be backed up with rational and cogent arguments.

victim ['vɪktɪm]

释义· *n.* 受骗者；上当的人；受害者；牺牲品

例句· 许多老年人是虚假广告的受骗者。

Many old people are victims of false advertising.

搭配· 受到某物的伤害　fall victim to sth.

fictitious [fɪk'tɪʃəs]

释义· *adj.* 虚构的；虚假的

例句· 这篇新闻报道的内容有一部分是虚构的。

The contents of this news report are partly fictitious.

同根· fictional *adj.* 虚构的；小说的

conduit ['kɑːnduɪt]

释义· *n.* （传递想法、新闻、金钱、武器等的）渠道；通道

例句· 互联网正在成为一种普遍的媒介，大部分信息都通过这个渠道流

向我们的眼、耳，进而进入我们的头脑。

The Internet is becoming a universal medium, the conduit for most of the information that flows through my eyes and ears and into my mind.

beset [bɪ'set]

释义 · *vt.* 困扰；使苦恼

例句 · 虚假广告一直困扰着消费者。

False advertising has been besetting consumers.

扩展 · beset（过去式）beset（过去分词）

documentary [ˌdɑːkjuˈmentri]

释义 · *n.* 纪录片 *adj.* 记录的；纪实的；文件的

例句 · 我决定通过一个电视纪录片来调研这个问题。

I decided to investigate the issue in a TV documentary.

搭配 · 纪录片 documentary film

comedy ['kɑːmədi]

释义 · *n.* 喜剧（片）；滑稽；幽默

例句 · 在我们观看喜剧时，很难忍住不笑。

It is difficult for us to refrain from laughing when we are seeing a comedy.

反义 · tragedy *n.* 悲剧；灾难

搭配 · 喜剧片 comedy film

glorify ['glɔːrɪfaɪ]

释义 · *vt.* 美化；吹捧；赞美

例句 · 媒体不应该过分美化名人。

The media should not overly glorify celebrities.

派生 · glorification *n.* 美化；颂扬

搭配· 自夸 glorify oneself

　　　颂扬爱国主义 glorify patriotism

pornographic [ˌpɔːrnə'ɡræfɪk]

释义· *adj.* 色情的；下流的

例句· 全国范围内打击色情网站的行动正如火如荼地进行。

The country's nationwide campaign to crack down on pornographic websites is in full swing.

同根· pornography *n.* 淫秽作品

overstate [ˌoʊvər'steɪt]

释义· *vt.* 夸大；言过其实

例句· 这些媒体无疑夸大了实情以吸引公众的注意力。

These media no doubt overstated their case with a view to catching the public's attention.

idol ['aɪdl]

释义· *n.* 偶像；神像

例句· 如今的许多偶像都是由娱乐节目制造出来的。

Many of today's idols are products made by entertainment programs.

派生· idolize *v.* 崇拜；热爱

搭配· 流行音乐偶像；足球明星；青少年的偶像 a pop/football/teen idol

worship ['wɜːrʃɪp]

释义· *n.* (U) 崇拜；崇敬 *v.* 崇拜；爱慕

例句· 偶像崇拜的社会风气与媒体的炒作密切相关。

The social atmosphere of idol worship is closely related to the media hype.

搭配· 拜金主义 money worship

偶像崇拜 idol worship

痴爱某人；极其崇拜某人 worship the ground sb. walks on

advertisement [ˌædvərˈtaɪzmənt]

释义· *n.* 广告；启事

例句· 音乐会筹办者在《纽约时报》上刊登了整版广告。

The organizers of the concert had taken out a full page advertisement in *The New York Times*.

同根· advertising *n.* 广告活动；广告业

搭配· 是……的典范 be an advertisement for sth.

商业广告 commercial advertisement

误导性广告 misleading advertisement

常 用 短 语

释义	短语
玷污名声	damage/taint/tarnish/sully one's reputation
夸大事实	blow things out of proportion
新闻自由	freedom of the press
突发新闻	breaking news
智力竞赛节目	quiz show
真人秀	reality show
脱口秀	talk show
肥皂剧	soap opera
满足不同口味	meet different tastes
公众人物	public figure
新闻道德	journalist ethics
小道消息	grapevine news
网红	online celebrity
审美疲劳	esthetic fatigue
大量的信息	a great deal of information
真实报道；真实记录	factual account
生活在虚拟世界里	live in a virtual world

侵犯某人的隐私	intrude on one's privacy
疯狂传播；像病毒般扩散	go viral
无名英雄	unsung hero
引人注目	in the limelight
易受负面影响	be susceptible to negative influences
道德准则	code of ethics
二手信息	second-hand information
模仿不良行为	copy undesirable behavior
高调的 / 低调的	high-profile/low-profile
老泡在电视机前的人；电视迷	couch potato
不健康的生活方式	unwholesome lifestyle

（巩）（固）（练）（习）

练习1 根据下面的中文释义，写出对应的单词（词组）。

A

捏造 f_____

新闻界 t_____

名人 c_____

流行 p_____

隐私 p_____

真人秀 r_____

公众人物 p_____

令人信服的 c_____

给……洗脑 b_____

炒作 h_____

偶像 i_____

B

受骗者 v_____

主流的 m_____

纪录片 d_____

透露 r_____

海报 p_____

美化 g_____

重大新闻 b_____

（报纸的）大字标题 h_____

收视率 r_____

耸人听闻的 s_____

时事 c_____

练习2 用方框中所给单词（词组）的适当形式填空。

disguise   censorship   violate   distort   worship
saturate with   overrate   delete   overstate   propaganda

1. The government today announced that press c_____（审查制度）was being lifted.

2. The media d_____（歪曲）reality; it categorizes people as all good or all bad.

3. This newspaper office is the government p_____ (宣传) machine.

4. The media regularly v_____ (侵犯) people's privacy.

5. In my opinion, Hirst's work has been vastly o_____ (高估).

6. She used a lot of news coverage to d_____ (掩饰) her shameful history.

7. The government has asked newspapers to d_____ (删除) stories about corruption.

8. Our culture is s_____ (使充满) television and advertising.

9. These media no doubt o_____ (夸大) their case with a view to catching the public's attention.

10. The social atmosphere of idol w_____ (崇拜) is closely related to the media hype.

☐ fabricate	☐ network	☐ indecent
☐ affair	☐ press	☐ flowery
☐ paparazzi	☐ witness	☐ bestseller
☐ celebrity	☐ subtitle	☐ audience
☐ sitcom	☐ edit	☐ poster
☐ censorship	☐ privacy	☐ commercialized
☐ sway	☐ violate	☐ billboard
☐ distort	☐ objective	☐ delete
☐ fraudulent	☐ headline	☐ reveal
☐ expose	☐ publication	☐ groupie
☐ widespread	☐ scandal	☐ whitewash
☐ subscribe	☐ relevance	☐ hype
☐ fame	☐ overrate	☐ mainstream
☐ popularity	☐ flyer	☐ episode
☐ issue	☐ addiction	☐ saturate
☐ newsworthy	☐ misleading	☐ digital
☐ coverage	☐ icon	☐ anecdote
☐ journal	☐ informative	☐ splash
☐ spotlight	☐ plot	☐ brainwash
☐ propaganda	☐ disguise	☐ cogent
☐ sensational	☐ impressionable	☐ victim
☐ rating	☐ vulgarity	☐ fictitious
☐ imperative	☐ premiere	☐ conduit
☐ medium	☐ theme	☐ beset

☐ documentary	☐ pornographic	☐ worship
☐ comedy	☐ overstate	☐ advertisement
☐ glorify	☐ idol	

表中共有 80 个单词

您不确认的单词 _____ 个，占总数的 _____%

如果比例高于 10%，请耐心再复习一遍。如果比例低于 10%，您可以开始下一章的托福写作之旅了！

写作高频替换词

动词 & 短语			
表明	☐ indicate	增长	☐ increase
	☐ reveal		☐ grow
	☐ suggest		☐ rise
	☐ show		☐ go up
	☐ prove		☐ enhance
	☐ demonstrate		☐ upsurge
	☐ bring out		☐ rocket
	☐ set forth		☐ mushroom
	☐ imply		☐ proliferate
认为	☐ consider		☐ sprout
	☐ suppose		☐ accelerate
	☐ deem		☐ soar
	☐ argue		☐ enlarge
	☐ maintain		☐ aggrandize

改善	☐ improve	支持	☐ support
	☐ ameliorate		☐ champion
	☐ amend		☐ advocate
	☐ rectify		☐ approve
	☐ redress		☐ back up
谴责	☐ condemn		☐ vote for
	☐ censure		☐ be in favor of
	☐ denounce	反对	☐ object (to)
	☐ reprimand		☐ oppose
	☐ decry		☐ raise objections
	☐ deprecate	促进	☐ promote
	☐ deplore		☐ improve
减少	☐ decrease		☐ enhance
	☐ lower		☐ facilitate
	☐ reduce		☐ upgrade
	☐ drop		☐ boost
	☐ decline	影响	☐ affect
	☐ diminish		☐ impact
	☐ cut down		☐ contribute to
	☐ shrink		☐ be a contributing factor to
	☐ curtail		☐ influence
恶化	☐ worsen	下降	☐ descend
	☐ deteriorate		☐ plummet
	☐ exacerbate		☐ plunge
	☐ aggravate		☐ slump

解决	□ address	阻碍	□ hinder
	□ settle		□ impede
	□ tackle		□ block
	□ solve		□ inhibit
	□ resolve		□ obstruct
	□ figure out	发展	□ develop
	□ cope with		□ boom
消除	□ eliminate		□ advance
	□ clear		□ evolve
	□ clear up		□ flourish
	□ remove	提高	□ raise
	□ take away		□ advance
	□ smooth away		□ enhance
获得	□ acquire		□ augment
	□ gain		□ develop
	□ achieve	遵守	□ obey
	□ obtain		□ abide by
	□ attain		□ comply with
成功	□ succeed		□ follow
	□ win	使迷惑	□ puzzle
	□ thrive		□ baffle
加快	□ accelerate		□ befuddle
	□ expedite		□ bewilder
	□ speed up		□ confound
	□ quicken		□ mystify

减轻	☐ ease	违反	☐ infringe
	☐ abate		☐ violate
	☐ lessen		☐ disobey
	☐ lighten		☐ transgress
	☐ relieve	允许	☐ allow
	☐ reduce		☐ permit
	☐ alleviate		☐ enable
	☐ mitigate		☐ give the means to
破坏	☐ damage	导致	☐ spark
	☐ wreck		☐ generate
	☐ destroy		☐ cause
	☐ ruin		☐ account for
	☐ jeopardize		☐ trigger
	☐ devastate		☐ give rise to
	☐ undermine		☐ bring about
开始	☐ commence		☐ lead to
	☐ initiate		☐ result in
	☐ begin	鼓励	☐ stimulate
	☐ start		☐ hearten
	☐ embark on		☐ encourage
耗尽	☐ deplete		☐ motivate
	☐ exhaust	误解	☐ misunderstand
	☐ use up		☐ misapprehend
	☐ run out of		☐ misinterpret
	☐ drain		☐ misread

保护	□ protect	建立	□ build up
	□ guard		□ establish
	□ defend		□ set up
	□ preserve		□ found
	□ conserve		□ take root
	□ shield		□ strike root
超过	□ surpass		□ install
	□ exceed	实现	□ achieve
	□ override		□ fulfill
	□ overwhelm		□ realize
	□ prevail		□ come true
	□ ranscend		□ accomplish
	□ be superior to	承认	□ concede
	□ outwit		□ admit
	□ outweigh		□ recognize
	□ outnumber		□ acknowledge
	□ forereach		□ accept

形容词 & 副词 & 短语			
程度大的	□ sufficient	严重的	□ severe
	□ considerable		□ serious
	□ extraordinary		□ grievous
	□ marked		□ acute
	□ exponentially		□ drastic

大量的	☐ enormous	重要的	☐ significant
	☐ abundant		☐ substantial
	☐ plentiful		☐ necessary
	☐ massive		☐ crucial
	☐ tremendous		☐ indispensable
	☐ considerable		☐ imperative
	☐ a great deal of		☐ irreplaceable
	☐ immense		☐ essential
	☐ substantial		☐ vital
	☐ numerous	贫穷的	☐ poor
特别地	☐ especially		☐ destitute
	☐ notably		☐ needy
	☐ particularly		☐ impoverished
富有的	☐ rich		☐ impecunious
	☐ wealthy	有益的	☐ beneficial
	☐ affluent		☐ helpful
	☐ deep-pocketed		☐ advantageous
传统的	☐ traditional		☐ favorable
	☐ conventional		☐ rewarding
	☐ orthodox	明显的	☐ manifest
	☐ old-fashioned		☐ distinct
大约	☐ approximately		☐ overt
	☐ almost		☐ obvious
	☐ nearly		☐ evident
	☐ roughly		☐ apparent

	☐ hazardous			☐ huge
	☐ adverse			☐ colossal
	☐ detrimental			☐ enormous
有害的	☐ destructive			☐ immense
	☐ baneful			☐ gargantuan
	☐ pernicious	巨大的		☐ grandiose
	☐ healthy			☐ massive
	☐ fit			☐ monolithic
健康的	☐ vigorous			☐ prodigious
	☐ robust			☐ titanic
	☐ wholesome			☐ tremendous
	☐ less			☐ unimportant
	☐ tiny			☐ marginal
小的	☐ diminutive			☐ peripheral
	☐ miniature	不重要的		☐ negligible
	☐ miniscule			☐ trifling
	☐ scarce			☐ trivial
	☐ meager			☐ complicated
	☐ scant			☐ intricate
稀少的	☐ scanty	复杂的		☐ complex
	☐ skimpy			☐ perplexed
	☐ sparse			☐ correct
	☐ frugal			☐ accurate
节俭的	☐ thrifty	正确的		☐ precise
	☐ economical			☐ proper

困难的	□ difficult	著名的	□ celebrated
	□ arduous		□ renowned
	□ strenuous		□ reputed
	□ daunting		□ distinguished
	□ formidable		□ illustrious
	□ exacting		□ prestigious
	□ insuperable		□ outstanding
	□ impassable		□ eminent
	□ onerous		□ notable
短暂的	□ transient		□ noticeable
	□ short-lived		□ striking
	□ ephemeral		□ remarkable
	□ transitory		□ preeminent

名词 & 短语			
名人	□ celebrity	专家	□ expert
	□ luminary		□ master
	□ legendary figure		□ specialist
环境	□ environment		□ professor
	□ setting		□ virtuoso
	□ surroundings	挫折	□ failure
	□ circumstance		□ frustration
	□ milieu		□ setback
	□ background		□ nonfulfillment

情况	□ story		□ difficult situations
	□ case		□ deadlock
	□ instance		□ impasse
	□ situation		□ stalemate
	□ condition	困境	□ dilemma
	□ circumstance		□ predicament
	□ status		□ quandary
	□ scenario		□ mire
特性	□ quality		□ morass
	□ feature		□ swamp
	□ trait		□ quagmire
	□ attribute		□ standstill
	□ characteristic		□ labyrinth
休闲娱乐	□ entertainment	精英	□ elite
	□ relaxation		□ meritocrat
	□ enjoyment	谜团	□ mystery
	□ recreation		□ puzzle
	□ pleasure		□ enigma
	□ leisure		□ conundrum
顶点	□ peak		□ riddle
	□ acme	有益的事物	□ antidote
	□ pinnacle		□ remedy
	□ climax		□ panacea
	□ apogee		□ boon
	□ zenith		□ blessing

混乱	☐ chaos	优点	☐ merit
	☐ confusion		☐ advantage
	☐ disorder		☐ virtue
	☐ mayhem	缺点	☐ drawback
	☐ disarray		☐ disadvantage
	☐ havoc		☐ shortcoming
	☐ turmoil		☐ defect

写作高分短语

释义	短语
大量的；无数的	a myriad of
A 取代 B	A serve as a substitute for B
对……做出解释；说明……的原因；（比例上）占	account for
有所成就；有所作为	amount to sth.
最多；充其量；在最好的情况下	at best
与某人争执	at odds with sb.
在危急关头；在危险中；成问题	at stake
决不是……	be anything but something
处于低潮；处于衰退状态	at a low ebb
受……的排挤	be elbowed aside by
充满	be laden with
被……取代	be superseded by
人才流失	brain-drains
极快的速度	breakneck pace
使……提前	bring forward

奉承；讨好；巴结	butter up
明白；认识到；时兴；流行	catch on
连锁反应	chain reaction
快速生产；大量生产	churn out
偶然遇见；使产生……印象	come across
有助于	conduce to
长久未解决的问题	continuing controversy
严厉打击；镇压	crack down
单调乏味的苦差事	donkeywork
构成……的主体	form the backbone of sth.
抽出时间做；终于去做	get around to
追求；追逐	go after
与……关系不大	have little bearing on
突然想出（主意或解决办法）	hit on
符合某事物；与某事物一致	in line with sth.
供应不足	in short supply
从长远来看；最终	in the long run
更不用说；不打扰	let alone
干涉	meddle in
处在……的边缘	on the brink of sth.
忙碌；奔波	on the run
一劳永逸地；彻底地	once and for all
掩盖，掩饰（分歧）	paper over
寄希望于某人 / 某物	pin one's hopes on sb./sth.
妨碍某人做某事	preclude sb. from doing sth.

紧迫的问题	pressing problem
拿钱投资于……	pump money into sth.
排除	rule out
与常理相悖	run contrary to common sense and daily experience
使某人（或自己）肩负重担	saddle sb./yourself with sth.
安然无恙	safe and sound
寻求；探求	seek to
慢而稳；稳扎稳打	slow and sure
不遗余力	spare no effort to
源于	spring/emerge/stem from
努力	strive to
冒险尝试	take the plunge
技术专家	tech whizz
人生的轨迹	the trajectory of a whole life
三管齐下的方法	three-pronged approach
使某人的未来充满不确定性	throw one's future into question
攻击；指责	throw stones at
岁月；时光	time and tide
迂回曲折	twist and turn
不良影响	unwelcome effects
带来经济增长	usher in economic growth
关于	with respect to

附录 3

参考答案

练习1

A: horizon versatile hypothesis interaction thesis curiosity
rote learning gifted vivid revise for overwhelm
B: competence diligent endeavor bias boarding student
differentiate virtue from evil supervise rigorous term mentor
primary/elementary school

练习2

1. appeals 2. diploma 3. ignored 4. generalists
5. obedience 6. proficient 7. indulged in 8. gone astray
9. provoked 10. undertake 11. discriminate 12. acute
13. deliberate 14. stifle 15. revise

练习1

A: persevere aptitude prosper accumulate compatible

morale interpersonal relationship yearn/long for attribute
demanding annual
B: high-paying job blue-collar compensate ambitious
work ethic endorse reputation bankruptcy strategy
a decent job determined

练习 2

1. announce 2. sacrificed 3. eminent 4. dismissed
5. painstaking 6. exert 7. strive for 8. enthusiastic
9. bargain with 10. resolve 11. adept at 12. convinced
13. resigned from 14. endorse 15. workaholic

第三章

练习 1

A: nutritious expenditure convenience remote reside
isolated estimate prospect shelter prevalent trend
food hygiene
B: esthetic dilemma tourist attraction/tourist spot permanent
recollection invigorated traffic jam/congestion entertainment
abstract domestic consumer

练习 2

1. accommodation 2. elaborate 3. inspiration 4. relatives
5. tempting 6. pursuit 7. encountered 8. prejudice against
9. endure 10. exhausted 11. spoiled 12. amuse
13. innate ability 14. puzzling over 15. prevail over

练习1

A: trustworthy   sagacious   sympathetic   defect   temperament
liability   solitary   catch up   aging society   extroverted   mutual
B: impetuous   generation gap   astute   sincere   organized
different world outlook   low-profile/low-key   betray   elegant
courteous   a tested friend/a friend in need/adversity

练习2

1. absurd   2. appreciate   3. bewilder   4. hesitant about
5. confide in   6. dynamic   7. depresses   8. fantastic
9. frustrated   10. considerate   11. notorious   12. satisfied with
13. suspicious of   14. sympathetic   15. indifferent

练习1

A: degrade   fossil   valid   conserve   foul   adjustment   pollutant
brutal   respiratory disease   global warming
heat-trapping gases/greenhouse gases
B: wildlife   contaminate   inhale   toxic   ecosystem   chronic
arable land   anthropogenic activities/human-related activities
poach   decompose   restore

练习 2

1. adapt   2. exceeded   3. disgrace   4. shortage
5. cruel   6. contribute to   7. altered   8. lessen
9. deplete   10. catalyst   11. disregarded   12. detriment
13. intolerable   14. mercy   15. discharged

第六章

练习 1

A: democracy   regulation   contemporary   foundation   welfare
health care   jeopardize   prohibit   incident   prerequisite
urban construction
B: aftermath   expand   a vicious circle   ethic   infrastructure
maintain   demolish   budget   stringent   intricate   impose

练习 2

1. abolish   2. establish   3. tackle   4. emerge
5. exaggerate   6. undergone   7. aggravated   8. interfere in
9. excluded   10. declared   11. demolish   12. curtail
13. shield   14. thrive   15. bribing

第七章

练习 1

A: universal   transaction   advanced   update   undermine
ride-hailing app   latest technology/cutting-edge technology
exploit   manual   simulate   paradise

B: in all walks of life proliferation anticipate alternative fantasy
ingenious novel apparatus unprecedented overshadow
curb

练习 2

1. utilize 2. surpass 3. track down 4. redundant 5. compute
6. substitute for 7. mitigate 8. breakthrough 9. terminated
10. converges 11. transformed into 12. symbol
13. accomplish 14. conscience 15. deprive

第八章

练习 1

A: fabricate the press celebrity popularity privacy
reality show public figure cogent brainwash hype idol
B: victim mainstream documentary reveal poster glorify
breaking news headline rating sensational current affairs

练习 2

1. censorship 2. distorts 3. propaganda 4. violates
5. overrated 6. disguise 7. delete 8. saturated with
9. overstated 10. worship